BEYOND Revival

It's Time For the Outpouring

Emanuel Vivian Duncan

Copyright © 2020 by Emanuel Vivian Duncan.

ISBN: Softcover   978-1-953537-03-4

All rights reserved. No part of this book may be reproduced or transmitted in any form or by any means, electronic or mechanical, including photocopying, recording, or by any information storage and retrieval system without express written permission from the author, except in the case of brief quotations embodied in critical reviews and certain other non-commercial uses permitted by copyright law.

Printed in the United States of America.

To order additional copies of this book, contact:
Bookwhip
1-855-339-3589
www.bookwhip.com

Table of Contents

Chapter 1: The Rationale 1

Chapter 2: Why Do Moves Of God Die? 9

Chapter 3: Life Saving Fuel For The Anointing Fire 63

Chapter 4: A Single Crop Or A Perpetual Harvest -
            The Choice Is Yours........................97

Chapter 5: It's Time For The Outpouring!.................124

Chapter 6: Liquid Power 140

Chapter 7: By My Spirit, Says The Lord!..................161

Appendix..195

The Rationale

What you are about to read is, by far, the longest and most detailed documentation, to date, of any prophetic revelation, which the Lord has been releasing to me over the years. In the main, these prophecies have unfolded on the principle of Prophetic Sequencing: the prophetic cycles or seasons through which the Lord continuously passes both the Church, in particular, and the world, at large, in the process of accomplishing His will in the earth.

The Lord has chosen this cycle as one in which to release a great volume of detailed revelation. This is clear evidence that we have come to a most important juncture in the history of the Church. His aim, at this time, is to equip His people so that we can make maximum impact upon the world. He also desires to get us ready to take our exit from the earth, as the Glorious Church, which He has always intended us to be in the first place. It is no wonder, then, that the Lord intends to take His people beyond the revival mentality and into a line of thinking that can accommodate and appropriate the ever-increasing outpouring of His Spirit, which He has promised, through Joel and Peter, for the end-time Church.

It is only under the showers of the outpouring and in the currents of the ensuing floods that we can receive the dimension of the anointing, which we will need to become the Glorious Church of which Apostle Paul speaks in Ephesians 5:27. Consequently, it stands to reason that by allowing us such detailed insight on the subject of the outpouring; God is ensuring that everyone lays hold of the truths that will govern life in the Kingdom in this season.

Yet, I do not for one moment purport that this is all that God has to say concerning this season. I am cognizant of the admonition that He gave to Elijah, in 1 Kings 19:18, pertaining to the fact that, at any given time, there may be seven thousand other prophets to whom He may be revealing His mind, on this or any of a million and one other issues. As such, one may need to hear from all seven thousand to get the complete picture. Even then, because of the dynamic nature in which God reveals Himself to us, we may still be found wanting, as far as capturing the entire scenario is concerned. Apostle Paul did caution us, in 1 Corinthians 13:9, that because, as human beings we only know in part, it is accepted that we can only prophesy in part.

What I do know, though, is that God has a unique way of condensing everything that He has to say, down to the personal level, tailoring it to fit one's experience and level of maturity. In this way, He guarantees that everyone is well positioned to grasp the truth. It means, then, that whatever a prophet says should really be just a stimulus to set us on our own personal quest to hear from God. The onus is upon each one, therefore, to go before God with the same burning passion that consumed David in Psalms 27:4: -

> One thing have I desired of the Lord, that will I seek after; that I may dwell in the house of the Lord all the days of my life, to behold the beauty of the Lord, and to inquire at his temple.

Yes, I have discovered that if there is anything that could take us beyond revival and position us under the showers of the outpouring, where God can continuously pour His Spirit into us, it will be this threefold passion expressed in the verse above:

- A passion for God's presence that I may dwell in the house of the Lord all the days of my life.

- A passion for worship - 'to behold the beauty of the Lord.
- A passion for God's word - 'to enquire in his temple.

Moreover, I make the following recommendations, in our quest to facilitate a clear grasp of the truths that are about to unfold.

- Read this prophetic communiqué prayerfully, allowing Holy Spirit to bear witness to your heart, concerning those concepts that may be difficult to understand.
- Apply the relevant truths to your situation so that your thinking and your actions become aligned to God's perspective on every issue in this season.
- Strive to understand the concept of Prophetic Sequencing. It will prove to be a very helpful tool in comprehending the rationale for labeling the moves of God in the Church and in the earth, at large, as prophetic cycles.

Prophetic Sequencing

If we can understand the essence of the relationship between the component parts of the wheel of an automobile and the mechanics by which they work, then, we will truly begin to grasp the phenomenon of Prophetic Sequencing. Traditionally, the wheel of an automobile is made up of a rim, a tube and a tire. Essentially, each component is a wheel in its own right, since it can roll along independently. Yet, none of them, on its own, can efficiently carry the automobile forward. All three of them must be properly assembled into one unit to accomplish this feat effectively. The tire must be set on the rim with the tube on the inside. The tube, in turn, must be inflated to the correct pressure for the automobile to move smoothly along. Speak to anyone who has had to ride home on a flat tire and he will most certainly verify this fact.

The Lord has revealed to me that, in essence, this is the same principle on which He takes His Church forward. He explained that even though in a given season, an outpouring of His Spirit may be powerful and revolutionary in its own right, it cannot, by itself, fully equip the Church for accomplishing its divine destiny and purpose. Loosely translated, it is not an end unto itself. As such, every time the Lord pours out of His Spirit upon His people, He does so based on foundation that has already been laid, as well as in preparation for the next wave of outpouring that will follow the current one.

Yes, everyone who is caught up in this current move of God must know that, as sure as the sun will rise tomorrow, another wave is on its way. It is incumbent on us all, then, to maximize and optimize but not fossilize this current flow, lest we miss out on the benefits of the next one that is forming on the horizon.

God is not concerned with who does or does not approve of the manner in which He moves within His Church or the pathway along which He decides to take it. When the season comes, i.e. in the fullness of time, He moves anyway. His two-fold purpose is to strengthen the Church and to make us ready for ruler ship, in this world and in the Kingdom to come.

Holy Spirit is the Executive Director of Operations, fiercely defending the interest of the Godhead in the Church. In his capacity as pneumatic the wind-he functions like the air in the tube to buoy things up and to set and keep the momentum of the season of the outpouring, as it unfolds, in much the same way that the wind used to blow huge sailing ships across the ocean in times past. Anywhere He is not allowed to direct proceedings the initial heightened excitement soon goes flat and the move loses its forward thrust. The result is that things become rough, the going gets tough and life in the Kingdom becomes frustrating for all involved.

The Lord has also used the analogy of ripples in a pool to further elucidate the principle of Prophetic Sequencing. When an object falls into a pool of water, the impact creates a series of concentric circles called ripples, which push outwards from the centre, in wave-like motion. As each ripple moves outward, it seems to spawn or give way to another from within itself. The entire arrangement appears to possess a type of dynamism, sustained by some unseen power, which no one can stop.

However, it is when one takes a still frame photograph of the unfolding ripples that one gets a true picture of the mechanics at work. What shows up is a series of rings set within one another; ever expanding in size from the centre to the perimeter. It creates a picture of wheels set within wheels. Such is the essence of Prophetic Sequencing.

When Holy Spirit is poured out upon the Church, there is, undoubtedly, a ripple effect. Wave after wave of God's glory just sweeps over His people "like the waters cover the sea" (Habakkuk 2:14). One revelation seems to spawn another and one season of prophetic release seems to emanate out of another, as the Father downloads His heart and mind into the spirits of those who continue to seek His face.

Those who allow themselves to get caught up in the ripples find themselves being swept along on a ride that gives them access to deep, hidden treasures of the Spirit. However, some have stood in its way, in their vain attempts to stop or, at best, retard its advance, only to find themselves being dragged along, involuntarily, by its swift moving current. Sadly, though, others have taken that very stance and have gotten crushed under the wheels of change. They were either ignorant of or had deliberately challenged the truth, which clearly warns that no legislation or doctrinal restriction can stem the flow of the tide of change.

I inquired of the Lord concerning a biblical precedent for this revelation on Prophetic Sequencing. Thereupon, He referred me to the account of His first encounter with Ezekiel. In that encounter, recorded in Ezekiel 1, He revealed Himself to the prophet as a "wheel in the middle of a wheel" (Ezekiel 1:16). He explained to me that what Ezekiel really saw was the ripple effect of His glory, being poured out upon the earth in prophetic time cycles or seasons.

Both the analogy of the composite nature of the wheel of an automobile and that of the ripples in a pool of water, coupled with the scriptural reference in Ezekiel 1:16 speak of the phenomenon of wheels within wheels, as the mechanics by which God pours out His Spirit upon the Church. Wheels always speak of forward motion and progress. It means, then, that when the Holy Spirit activates a new wave of God's glory within the Church, the purpose is to take the Church forward. For example, there is a greater purpose for the outpouring of the apostolic and prophetic anointing upon the Church, in recent years, than simply for one to claim that he is a prophet or an apostle. The true divine purpose for such a move is the advancement of the Kingdom of God and not necessarily for the promotion and aggrandizement of individuals and their ministries.

So, here comes another wave of God's glory that will duly establish itself in orbit within the atmosphere of the Church. Having done so, it will produce power to propel the Church forward. Like in Elijah's day, what began as a man's hand (all five elements of the five-fold ministry gifts now being in operation in the Church) is expanding into a heavy cloud cover over the Church. Soon this cloud will break and unleash a shower of anointing, so impacting, that both the Church and the world, at large, will see and acknowledge God's glory being revealed, as the waters cover the sea.

For those whose spiritual receivers are tuned to God's prophetic frequency, already we can hear the thundering voice of the God of Glory and the joyful sounds of an abundance of rain, coming from within the clouds. We can see the flashing light of the qaran—the rays of God's glory similar to that which shot from the face of Moses-piercing the darkness of spiritual ignorance and tradition, like bolts of lightning on a dark, stormy night. When this cloud bursts, it will usher in a new prophetic cycle. The spiritual experience will be like being caught in the path of the lava flow of a perpetual, massive, volcanic eruption in the natural. In much the same manner, waves and waves of the anointing will fall upon and flow through the Church in ever increasing torrents. Nothing and no one will be able to stop or retard its advance or control its flow. It will be a choice of Jump in; Get sucked in or Burn!'

So, fasten your seat belt and get excited, because you are about to take a ride upon the wheel in the middle of the wheel, which will usher you into a state of existence called Beyond Revival. It is there that you will hear the Holy Spirit declare, "It's time for the Outpouring!"

Here is a song that I wrote that captures the essence of this season of the Outpouring:

THE SOUND OF ABUNDANCE

There's a sound of abundance of rain,

Coming over the mountains and plains.

It's becoming increasingly clear,
As it gathers ever so near.

Chorus:

Break up, break up your fallow ground!

Open; open your hungry soul.

And let God fill your heart with waters from on high!

"Be careful-watch out for attacks from Satan, your great enemy. He prowls around like a hungry, roaring lion, looking for some victim to tear apart" (1Peter 5:8, TLB).

Why Do Moves Of God Die?

$\mathcal{B}$ased on careful research, Church historians have given a window of only three to five years from the onset to the demise of a move of God. However, it is my firm conviction that the release of the anointing, in this cycle, will defy historical trends in terms of duration and magnitude. It is a flow that will gather momentum in the lives of individuals and ministries who set themselves to walk in harmony with the will of God.

In religious literature, a move of God is commonly referred to as a REVIVAL. Ignorantly, it has also crept into the everyday speech of the Church. It is not uncommon to hear many ministers instruct their congregations to pray and fast for the Lord to send revival. Others have been heard to say, for years, that a revival is coming. Still others spend their days longing for the revivals of yesteryear. A high percentage actually hold at least one set of revival services every year, while others hold one for every season of the year. However, my question is this: "What has happened to the fire of God's glory that was ignited within the assembly during the Spring Revival, a mere three months or so ago, now that the Summer Revival is being billed as the one event that will bring back God's glory to the church?"

You see, what such Church leaders do not realize is that there is a death factor intrinsically built into the use of the term, revival, as a label for identifying a move of God. The term, REVIVAL, literally refers to the act of bringing back to life that which is dead. The truth is that, since the dead has to be brought back to life, the presupposition is that it was once alive. Consequently, the key questions that beg to be answered are:

- Why did the move of God die?
- Who killed it?
- Was there an accident or some fatal disease that attacked it?
- Was there sabotage?

Even more indictable: Was there carelessness on the part of those who were responsible for keeping it alive? Why would God want to resurrect a move, when He knows that those who let the previous one die may do so again?

If we were to answer these questions honestly, we will be able to determine what became of the twentieth century Church movements, such as, the Azusa Street Revival, the Healing Movement and the Word of Faith Movement, just to name a few. What is absolutely encouraging, though, is that the Lord has declared that this prophetic cycle, into which we have entered, will now take the Church BEYOND REVIVAL into a dimension called THE OUTPOURING. This one does not have to die like the others. However, we must learn from what happened in the past and be willing to follow His instructions specific to this new season.

It has never been God's desire to have to come visiting His Church, time after time, to re-establish movements and rekindle fires, in response to the prayers of His people. His original intent, even from the day of Pentecost, was to have one continuous movement, ever increasing in momentum and intensity, which would take His Church from one stage of glory to another. In the process, He would fashion His people into a formidable bulwark against the advancement of the Kingdom of darkness. Paul encapsulates this original intent of God in 2 Corinthians 3:18, AMP:

And all of us, as with unveiled face, (because we) continued to behold (in the Word of God) as in a mirror the glory of the Lord, are constantly being transfigured into His very own image in ever increasing splendor and from one degree of glory to another; (for this comes) from the Lord (Who is) the Spirit.

Revival Fire

The common imagery that typifies revival is that of a blaze of fire. Many who pray and fast for it are often heard to cry, "Lord, send the fire!" When it does come, the commentators usually report that there is an outbreak of revival fire in this place or that. Yet, what most of the Church has not been cognizant of is the fact that encoded in the analogy of fire as the nature, scope and function of revival, is a grave, divine mandate to keep the flames alive.

God does not want us to just obtain the fire as an end unto itself. He is equally interested in us sustaining and retaining it. The Church must adopt the policy that whatever we obtain, we must maintain in order to retain.

What, then, is the vital principle, which we need to observe, to enable us to build the revival fire from a spark to an ever-expanding, ever-intensify ing, raging inferno that will never go out? The key is in understanding the nature of fire as a natural phenomenon.

The basic principle on which fire operates is this: Fire needs fuel. Manufacturers have taken this into consideration in the way that they have constructed the stove. In the process, they have also committed all users to adhere to this principle, if they are to maximize the use of the appliance.

The basic set of mechanics, on which a gas stove operates, is that, on the flat upper surface of a metal frame, there are openings in which burners are placed. Each burner is attached to a narrow, metal pipeline, which is joined to a larger one, coming in from the street or attached to a gas cylinder, nearby. The line from the street and the one from the gas cylinder represent a source of high concentration from which fuel flows to the burners, not only to produce a flame, but also to sustain it, when it is obtained. To manage the life and intensity of the flames, there is a control panel, carrying a dial, calibrated from low to high, designated to each burner. As long as the dial is set between low and high the fuel line is open and the flame stays alive. However, as soon as the dial is turned to the 'off' position, the flame dies.

Consequently, no one in his right mind, ever ignites the burner of a gas stove, then immediately turns the dial to the 'off position, and yet expects water to boil or food to be cooked. Once ignited, the flames on the burner need fuel to keep on burning. This fuel must keep flowing to the burner, without impediment, from a source where it is in high concentration. The intensity of the flame, at the burner, is in direct proportion to the amount of fuel that is flowing to it.

Here, then, is the simple but vital principle that governs the ignition and maintenance of any type of fire: When fire is obtained, you must maintain the flow of fuel being fed to it, in order to retain or sustain the flame. Do this and you will have no need to start the process all over again or to seek to rekindle or revive the flame.

I am sure that, right now, your spiritual antennas are tingling with a prophetic download, which is entering your system, pertaining to revival fire. If, then, we dare to refer to the sudden release of the anointing as revival fire, then, we most definitely need to consider, comprehend and apply the above law to it.

When an individual or a congregation earnestly seeks the face of God for a release of anointing fire, God usually responds by doing so. Matthew 5:6 teaches that those who hunger and thirst for righteousness will be filled with the very righteousness, which they seek. In essence, it happens along the same vein as when one scratches a match and puts it to a burner. As long as gas is flowing to it, a flame will ignite. Once that initial burst of anointing fire explodes within one's spirit or erupts in the midst of a congregation, it is incumbent upon the recipients that they feed it with the right fuel, not only to bring it from a spark to a flame, but also to maintain it, as such, until it becomes a raging inferno.

What is this fuel? It is a mixture of the very prayer, praise, worship, repentance, fasting, forgiveness, covenant-type interpersonal relationships, hunger for holiness, meditation on the Word of God and the yearning for God's presence that marked the period of seeking, before the fire came. The truth is that the longevity and intensity of the anointing fire are directly proportionate to the measure to which people are willing to continue observing the above principles. At the same time, though, they must be willing to incorporate the new things that the Lord may introduce along the way.

I know that the question that begs for an answer, at this time, is this: "If it is so simple, why, then, do revivals die?" The plain truth is that revivals die because, in general, the Church does not take heed to Peter's admonition in I Peter 5:8, NIV:

> Be self-controlled and alert. Your enemy the devil prowls around like a roaring lion looking for someone to devour.

We must understand that, in ordinary times, the devil does not only hate the Church, but is also mortally afraid of it. If this is so, then, one does not need much imagination to perceive the depth of confusion and consternation into which he descends, when an assembly or individual is in the throes of an explosion of anointing fire.

Satan knows that the Church, bathed by waves of red hot anointing, poses the greatest threat to his operations in the earth. He becomes disturbed by the new commitment to righteous living, the fresh fervor for winning the lost, the intensification in spiritual warfare against witchcraft and the greater manifestation of the power of God for miracles, signs and wonders. He knows that this new fervor will only make the Church more militant and lead it to mount more powerful assaults against his ascendancy over the affairs of the earth.

Consequently, Satan takes a decision to snuff out the fire at all cost. In pursuit of this, he launches an all out campaign against the move of God, attacking both its leaders and followers and seeking to discredit every principle or truth that fuels the move. The truth is that Satan has a thousand and one devices that he uses in this campaign. The key to survival is in being able to recognize them.

When we are able to detect and decipher Satan's devices, it will not only facilitate the building of strong defenses, but also, equip us to mount effective counter offensives against him. God wants us to know this because it is God's desire "To keep Satan from getting the advantage over us; for we are not ignorant of his wiles and intentions." (2 Corinthians 2:11, AMP).

Here, now, is a short list of the master spirits that Satan recruits in his efforts to unleash an all out attack against the Church or individual, when anointing fires breakout. We will also unmask their line of attack and area of specialization.

Bear in mind, though, that we are not clay pigeons in a shooting gallery, waiting to be picked off by these spirits. Rather, we are well equipped with spiritual weapons to resist and repel them and, in turn, to launch offensives of our own against their ranks.

It will be to the advantage of every individual, every leader and every congregation, therefore, to regard the following segment as a virtual communiqué from Jesus, the Commander-in-Chief, at Central Command, to all soldiers of the Kingdom. It is aimed at setting us on a war footing to stoutly defend hard-earned releases of the anointing that God chooses to pour out upon us, as one season gives way to another. So, besides reading them carefully, why not make a concerted effort to follow the instructions inscribed therein.

With the onset of the initial explosion, which heralds the first prophecy, the first healing, the first large intake of souls and/or the first wave of supernatural manifestations, there arises a sense of great excitement and accomplishment among the leadership and people of a congregation. The natural outflow from this should be an intensification of the quest for more of God. What happens more often than not, though, is just the opposite. Sometime after the initial euphoria, that very sense of achievement seems to act as a sleeping pill that could ever so slowly lull an individual, a congregation and even an entire organization into deep slumber. This is when the spirit called Complacency swings into high gear.

Complacency creates the feeling that now that we have what we had been waiting on for so long, everything is alright. As such, we do not need to be as fervent in prayer or as diligent in meditating on the Word or as vigilant concerning the nature and scope of inter-personal relationships or as passionate for the presence of God, as during the days, when everyone was seeking the face of God for a new move of the Spirit. It causes a congregation to begin to worship the worship experience, instead of worshipping God, who is the object of worship and who grants the experience by His sovereign will, in the first place. It dupes one into switching the focus from winning souls to counting souls. Moreover, it entices leadership to be more concerned about creating the right public image than in prevailing upon the people to be transformed into the image of God.

Oh no! This does not happen right away, say within a year or even within two. Complacency is too smart a spirit for that. He knows that, within those early days, everyone is on guard. What he uses to his advantage, however, is his knowledge of human nature. He knows that the average human being gets involved in an activity for the short term, but hardly for the long haul, even in an experience as euphoric as a move of God. He is well aware that eventually human beings either begin to rest on their laurels or lose their interest in and their enthusiasm for the goings-on.

A strong case in point is found in Revelations 2:4, which records the Lord's only complaint against the Church at Ephesus. He did not accuse it of going into apostasy, idolatry or anything so blatant. He reprimanded it for having lost its first love. In a manner of speaking, it had become complacent.

Whenever complacency strikes, the anointing fire eventually dies a natural death. It lulls the people into a state of feeling that they have arrived and, as such, they do not need to be as vigilant as before, in maintaining an adequate flow of fuel to feed the fire. As said before, commentators expect this to occur within three to five years of the initial explosion.

Yet, complacency is not the only problem. In fact many people who have experienced major moves of God have become aware of the statistics and have made the smart move of actually appointing keepers of the flame. They are the intercessors whose spirits are like thermometers, constantly taking the temperature readings of the fire and sounding the alarm, whenever they sense a drop in fervency.

However, there are times when other spirits slip in unnoticed. By the time they are detected, in most cases, they have managed to do irreparable dam age to the fire, even while people are on the lookout against Complacency. One must remember that these spirits operate in gangs and have a million and one disguises at their disposal. Therefore, we must be sober and vigilant and ask the Lord to teach us how to discern both the presence and the methodologies of these spirits whose desire is to snuff out the anointing fire for which God's people have been interceding for many years.

Extremism

When Extremism attacks, he brings along spookiness, ignorance and heresy, as part of his gang.

Together, they succeed in generating fear among people, since they manage to influence leadership into instituting a program of subtle or, sometimes, blatant mind control over a congregation. This is usually done under the guise of having a directive from the Lord.

Then, there is the case of people being duped into making crazy, unintelligent decisions such as occurred during the move of God, in the late sixties/ early seventies, called the Faith Movement. Based on the teachings of the day, many people became so super spiritual that they refused to seek medical attention, even for chronic diseases. People were being taught that it would show a lack of faith in God for one to go to a doctor. Of course, no one stopped to ask, "If going to the doctor was wrong, is it possible for one to be a doctor and still be a Christian?" Needless to say, many people suffered unduly and some even went to an untimely grave because of such extremism.

The teachings needed to be balanced with the fact that there are times when God uses doctors as the extension of His healing hands. It might have also helped a great deal, if they had taken time to find out why Jesus would call himself the Great Physician.

Extremism also shows its ugly head in other areas such as dress and inter-personal relationships. I remember a case where a strong move of God began in a particular assembly after many years of praying and fasting. The pastor's response was to set a rule, banning any female from entering the sanctuary without her head covered. A sign over the front door advised that mantillas will be provided for those women who had no hats or head ties of their own.

It was a sight to see what happened every time the Holy Spirit moved through the sanctuary. As these women began to dance and jump, under the anointing, the first thing to go was their hats and mantillas. Whenever this occurred, they would actually come out of the spirit, stop their dance; retrieve and reposition their hats, mantillas or head ties, then, enter the spirit again to dance and sing. This would take place on several occasions, for as long as the praise and worship session lasted. What a travesty!

For his part, as the move of God gathered momentum, the pastor adopted the practice of ensuring that he tied a white silk chord around his waist, every time he was ready to minister the word of God. His rationale was that he must put on the belt of truth, if he is to speak the truth of God effectively. In addition to this, he designated the platform and the carpeted area immediately in front of it as holy ground. As such, anyone entering that area had to take off his or her shoes, like both Moses and Joshua had to do, when they met the Lord. How extreme can one get!

Needless to say, because of Extremism, more energy was spent on ensuring that hats were on the heads of the women and not enough on transformation of their hearts. In spite of the measurable, tangible presence of God, in the congregation, gossip and confusion marked the nature of the inter-personal relationships among the people. Eventually, many people withdrew their membership, distraught and wounded, as a result of slander and character assassination. While some attached themselves to other congregations, many have not even cared to continue serving the Lord. Sadly, the move of God fizzled out and, no doubt, those who remained are now fasting and praying for God to do it again. One wonders what guarantees they are giving to God that they will not kill it again, if He does so.

Sabotage

Sabotage is another spirit that attacks and kills revivals. His mode of attack is multi-pronged. One of the first lines of attack is to raise up self-appointed leaders of the move of God. In the majority of cases, these would-be leaders are either initially indifferent or skeptical towards the new move, although they were part of the ministry, during the time of seeking God for the fire and were eye witnesses of its arrival. Others arrive on the scene, just when things have sprung into full gear. What both sets of people have going for them is the power of influence and charisma that they so skillfully use as leverage to win the unsuspecting over to their side.

In the case of the former group, they are quite often mere onlookers during the period leading up to the outbreak of the anointing fire. They take little or no part in the initial periods of prayer and fasting. They also do not see it necessary to undergo the degree of attitude adjustment and inner cleansing through which the rest of the congregation goes. They consider themselves as being intrinsically righteous. Their pride and self-righteousness keep them standing proudly on their feet, when others are on their faces before God.

What further compounds the situation is the fact that such persons are usually smart, intelligent, and well-positioned on their jobs. Additionally, many are extremely successful at business. However, while others are at the altar, seeking the face of God, they are in libraries and on the internet, researching the history of past revivals. At the first sign of the outbreak of anointing fire, they emerge from the sidelines, purporting to possess the keys to proper management of the move of God. However, such individuals make the fatal error of confusing some formula that they have created out of their research with access to the Father by way of the uncompromising principle of faith.

Sadly, though, many God-appointed leaders feel intimidated by this aura of academia and willingly provide these researchers with a platform to speak. It soon becomes painfully clear to all those who are spiritually sensitive that what these researchers are pouring into the fire is not fuel but flame-choking foam, from their intellectual fire extinguishers. If leadership does not make decisive moves to rein them in, within reasonable time, it may prove to be too late to salvage any embers from the fire, after these researchers are done with their maneuvers.

The other line of attack, which the spirit of Sabotage uses, comes through people who arrive on the scene after the move of God is already in full swing. They come professing either to be veterans of past moves of God or to have just visited some ongoing move somewhere. Their line of attack is to attempt to impose upon the present move a Xeroxed or duplicate version of what they experienced in the past or of what they observed in the place from which they have just come. Either way, such a proposal is always potentially detrimental to the present move.

One must understand that when God releases Holy Ghost fire upon a people, it is always in response to the fervent cry of the collective heart of that people. In that case, He fashions it to meet their needs and to fit into the geographical and cultural setting of that people. So, for one to attempt to make a wholesale imposition of the goings-on of one era or in one location upon the proceedings of another is to attempt to rob God of both His creativity and credibility, as far as answering the specific cry of His people, in a specific locale, is concerned.

Of course, this in no way preempts the fact that events and occurrences of a similar nature may happen in moves of God in different locations and in different eras. However, such a phenomenon must be the sole prerogative of the Holy Spirit, the Executive Director of all moves of God in the earth. It must never be as a result of misdirected enthusiasm.

Should we, then, not read up on moves of God of the past or visit those of the present, as we seek God for the release of the anointing in our own lives and locale? Of course, we should! What, then should we look for when we do so? We should:

- Identify the principles and practices, which the particular congregation adopted, in the lead up to the outbreak.
- Recognize and strive to avoid the mistakes that might have derailed the progress of past revivals.
- Identify and steer clear of the pitfalls that may be slowly gnawing away at the foundations of current revivals.

To do otherwise is to invite the spirit of Sabotage to take a hard-earned move of God for a ride over a cliff, causing it to die an untimely death.

This spirit of Sabotage is not a new phenomenon. It has been around for as long as God has been engineering new moves of the Holy Spirit in the earth. When God made the move to revive the earth, as recorded in Genesis 1–3, Sabotage was right there in Eden to short circuit the relationship between man and God. It showed up again in Jerusalem, in the persons of Samballat and Tobiah, when the Holy Spirit commissioned Nehemiah to rebuild the walls that had been broken down. The plan did not work, however, because Nehemiah recruited an army of people who "had a mind to work." (Nehemiah 4:6). Sabotage again showed up in the New Testament, when the Holy Spirit used Apostle Paul to ignite anointing fire among the Gentiles. His attempts to apply damage control measures and to rekindle dampened fires form the basis of most of his epistles to the various churches.

Very notable among the many devastating attacks that the spirit of Sabotage launched, in Paul's era, was the one directed against the Church at Galatia. In that attack, Sabotage mutated itself into legalism to 'pervert the gospel of Christ.' The effects of that attack were so devastating to the spirit and psyche of the people that Paul had to apply shock treatment to jumpstart the move of God one more time. Galatians 3:1 records the drastic move that Paul was forced to make, in his effort to mount an effective counter offensive against Sabotage and legalism, "O foolish Galatians, who hath bewitched you that you should not obey the truth? Are you so foolish? Having begun in the Spirit are ye now made perfect by the flesh?"

Today, the warning remains the same to all who would dare to rattle the gates of Heaven, in quest of a move of God, whether individually or corporately. Be on the lookout for the bewitching spirit of Sabotage that could so soon strangle the baby that you have travailed so long and hard to bring forth.

Character Assassination

The modus operandi of this spirit is to defame the character of the leaders of the move by raising questions, pertaining to their true agenda, especially in the areas of finances and relationship with members of the opposite sex. Slander, Gossip and Rumor Mongering are the directors of operations, in such cases. What is so disturbing is the fact that, in the midst of a mighty move of God, where the accent is on holiness and purity of the inner man, these spirits are never hard pressed to find willing human agents within the very congregation, to carry out their dirty work.

As soon as such human agents are located, these spirits assign them the task of gathering and broad casting information about past indiscretions of certain leaders. Of necessity, they pay very little attention to verifying the authenticity of the information or whether the individuals in question, have made a 180° turn away from the particular practices. They bank on exploiting a weakness, innate in the human being—that tendency to readily and unquestioningly accept negative news about others, especially those in leadership, whether in the secular world or in the Church.

Slander, Gossip and Rumor Mongering function on the premise that they can bring any move of God to a grinding halt by striking the shepherd and having the sheep scatter. They know that as soon as rumors begin to circulate, the image of the leader becomes distorted in the eyes of the followers. Since people are not as forgiving as God is, the expected outcome is that they will leave the church or organization in disgust. Once the exodus begins, the move loses momentum and dwindles out into oblivion. You see, it is an infallible truth that, in the same way that people perish for a lack of vision, so too does a vision perish for a lack of people.

What every leader needs to know is that, in the lead up to the outbreak of Holy Ghost fires in a ministry, he must examine his own life with a view to committing to the fire of God's altar, every practice, habit and attitude that is contrary to God's law. When he walks away from the altar, he must vow not to return to them. Instead, he must be willing to make a covenant with God to do what is right. By the time the glory fires break out, Slander and his gang will be hard pressed to make rumors stick because God will rise to his defense.

On their part, the people must learn how to guard themselves against becoming agents of death, destroying the very move of God for which they fasted and prayed all these years. They must establish covenant together to be committed to the vision of their leaders, even in the face of a mountain of evidence against them.

Burn Out

This spirit clouds the vision, so that, in an effort to be super spiritual, the individual or ministry crosses the line of what is physically, mentally or socially proper. Here are a few glaring examples:

The Burn Out Spirit leads an individual to over indulge in fasting, precipitating grave digestive and other physical complications. I remember being in a meeting at which this grossly overweight prophet was ministering. He sensed that people were quizzical about his weight, so he set out to explain why it was so. He related to us, weeping bitterly as he did so, how he wanted so much of the anointing in the early days of the call of God on his life that he would fast for weeks on end.

Oh yes, he did hook up to a higher level anointing, but he also damaged the glands that regulate his metabolism. He lamented that, short of a miracle, no amount of dieting or exercise program can correct the problem. He admonished the congregation to guard against similar occurrences in our lives by allowing wisdom to prevail.

The Burn Out Spirit chides anyone who, in an effort to nourish the body, takes a meal out of turn and labels him as being weak in 'flesh'. That per son now walks around with a cloud of condemnation over him and a feeling of guilt on the inside, both of which can eventually choke the fuel line and cause the anointing fires to burn out.

Another major line of attack that the Burn Out Spirit launches against a move of God is to create the illusion that you cannot get enough of a good thing. Thus, ministries are duped into practicing improper time management. There are daily morning and evening prayer meetings, weekly all night warfare sessions and the too-frequently-held 'revival, deeper life or consecration campaigns that, sometimes, run for weeks on end.

Leadership gives little or no thought to the fact that it is the same set of people who are expected to attend and/or serve in these sessions, night after night. Lost in the mix is the fact that these people also have obligations at home, at work, at school or in their businesses. The result is that the frequency of the meetings places heavy strains on both the corporate body and on the individual. For example:

- The human, material and financial resources of the ministry are heavily taxed, resulting in many ardent followers dropping out, facilities having to be frequently repaired or replaced because of wear and tear, thus depleting finances.
- Relationships in the home suffer a heavy toll, because many people rush to church without adequately seeing to the needs of their spouses and children. I have known of many instances in which children have gone astray and marriages have broken down because of such lack of wisdom.
- Both leaders and members have experienced health problems because of the beating that the body takes from having to attend services so often and on such a prolonged basis.
- Many have been sanctioned by their superiors or have even lost their jobs because of decline in the standard of their performance or from sleeping on the job, due to tiredness brought on by the all-too-frequent night sessions.

The Burn Out Spirit knows that when revival fires are blazing high, it is hardly likely that leader ship or the people will succumb to the enticement to act immorally, incurring judgment from God. Yet, it also knows that no human being can fire on all cylinders perpetually. Since the fire does not burn in a vacuum, but needs human beings to be both its carriers, as well as its keepers, as long as it can get us to burn our bodies out, we will sooner or later be rendered incapable of going for the long haul. Thus, the fire will eventually die anyway just as if judgment had befallen the revival due to immorality or some other sin.

Between 1995 and 2001, there was a mighty, raging inferno of anointing fire burning in Pensacola, Florida. People were traveling from far flung areas of the globe just to witness the spectacle and be part of the experience. Sadly, today, as I write, it is no more. That fire blazed for almost seven years, but, could not withstand a broadside attack from the Burn Out Spirit.

In an effort to maximize the anointing, for almost all of that period, there was at least one service every weekday and, several on weekends, running consecutively from early morning to way into the night. It was truly a case of firing on all cylinders. At that rate, burn out soon set in. People became weary. Families came under great strain, resulting in broken homes, even divorces and juvenile delinquency.

What should a ministry do then, so as to counteract the Burn Out Spirit at the onset of a move of God? The first thing is for leadership to know that the anointing fire is really evidence of the presence of God in that particular locale. God has promised to enthrone Himself in the praises of His people. He has also promised that wherever and whenever His people gather together, in His name, He will be there in their midst. The correct deduction, therefore, is that a ministry does not have to gather everyday for God to be in their midst. Yet, the people can be assured that whenever they gather, He will be there. The wise thing to do, then, would be to maintain the regular schedule of services and conduct special nightly or daily sessions for short periods, from time to time.

In essence, accessing the glory fire follows the same procedure as what the manufacturers of the stove have set in place. They do not expect the burners to be alight perpetually. Yet, they also understand that the average user does not relish the idea of always having to strike a match or flick a lighter every time he needs to use his stove. Consequently, they have placed a low, continuously burning flame, called a pilot light, deep inside the stove. The system of lines that bring fuel to the burner is all connected to it. Therefore, as soon as a dial is turned on, the designated burner bursts into flames, as the fuel becomes ignited by the pilot light. Leadership and members alike of any ministry, caught in the flames of anointing fire, can learn a world of valuable lessons from this, as it pertains to repulsing attacks from the Burn Out Spirit.

Everyone should understand that the real flames of glory burn, not in a vacuum existing somewhere in the atmosphere of the sanctuary, but rather, deep in the hearts of the people involved. Therefore, in much the same way as the pilot light works, the sanctuary can burst into flames every time they gather. For this to happen, each one will have to ensure that he continuously fuels the flame burning in his own spirit, while away from the sanctuary—at home, on the job, in the malls and so on. He can do his praying without ceasing, worshiping in his spirit and choosing to do right in the sight of God, all day long. Then, when the church gathers together, all that will be needed is for the preacher, the worship minister, the intercessor or someone of that nature, to open the fuel line with a 'Hallelujah!', a 'Praise the Lord!' or the release of a new revelation from the word of God. The result will be that the flames of passion for God's presence (pilot lights), burning deep within the spirit of each worshipper will ignite and come together to turn that sanctuary into a raging inferno. In that way, the Burn-Out Spirit can never gain a foothold in that place

Unhealthy Competition

This spirit causes a move of God to come down with a chronic case of "the-keeping-up-with-and-out doing-the-Jones' Syndrome". It dupes people into assessing the temperature of the fire in their own ministry by comparing it with what is happening elsewhere. If it is not as hot as the neighbor's, then, they add imported fuel. If it is hotter, then, they may sit back and become complacent and proud. Either way this could derail the move because the only true source of fuel for the continued life of a move of God is adherence to the will of God for that move.

Every individual or ministry caught up in a move of God must take cognizance of the fact that one's righteousness is not determined by the extent of the righteousness or unrighteousness of another individual or ministry. It must always be measured against the standard set by the Word of God and by God's will for that individual or for that ministry.

Witchcraft/Manipulation

This Spirit has two major lines of attack. First, it deceives people into taking their focus from the Lord, the provider of anointing fire, and placing it on the human beings who are leading the move of God. Inevitably, traces of virtual idol worship begin to appear in the ministry, as people, with little or no protest on the part of the maximum leader, inadvertently and sometimes deliberately, create an atmosphere of cultism around him. Such people need to acquaint themselves with Isaiah 42:8, KJV, which issues this grave warning to all and sundry: "I am the Lord: that is my name: and my glory will I not give to another..."

If left unchecked, such a practice, in turn, renders the congregation susceptible to manipulation, intimidation and control by any or all of their leaders who may not have made the appropriate character adjustments, in the lead up to the outbreak of Holy Ghost fire. Wherever this diabolical trio operates, witchcraft flourishes with impunity.

Over the years, the Lord has proven to us, by many infallible proofs, that if a man's character does not outweigh his charisma, he can be a ticking time bomb, set to explode with the slightest agitation. He may take on the persona of a dictator, using the authority that the anointing brings to wield unhealthy control over the congregation. Such a leader is usually unrestrained in the way that he publicly berates anyone who dares to show the slightest opposition to his authority, even going to the extent of unceremoniously excommunicating the offender from the congregation.

On the flipside of the same coin, a leader who is high on charisma but short on character can also become a pied piper who may virtually hypnotize people and lead them any which way with his smooth tongue, suave looks and winsome personality. All that he needs is a well-placed 'Thus saith the Lord!' as a preamble to his deliberations, and he will almost always succeed in enticing people to do his bidding. Sadly, he succeeds at this, even when the victims know, in their heart of hearts, that such actions are contrary to God's will. Anyone who objects or asks probing questions is deemed a troublemaker and labeled an outcast.

If there are no systems in place to establish checks and balances on either of the two personas described above-dictator and pied piper—the results can be devastating to both the move of God and to the people of that congregation. Manipulation rules the roost, spawning persecution of innocent people, on the one hand, and misdirected hero worship, on the other. This is what causes a move of God that began in truth to deteriorate into the error of cultism and eventually fade away into oblivion. Think about the Jim Jones tragedy! Is it possible that God had truly entrusted him with a genuine anointing? Could it be that his high-level charisma drew the people but his low-level character destroyed them? Just asking!

The other angle of attack that the spirit of Witchcraft Manipulation mounts against a move of God is to actually cause practicing witches and war locks to infiltrate the movement. Satan knows the great havoc that a genuine move of God can wreak upon his Kingdom of darkness. His intent, therefore, is to stop it at all cost or, at least, render it ineffective. Consequently, he encourages these agents of death to come into a ministry, disguised as bona fide converts or transfers from other gatherings.

As soon as these persons gain a measure of acceptance, by winning the confidence of both the leader ship and the people, they usually vie for and manage to take control of key areas of ministry in the assembly. Their most prized targets are intercession, worship, administration and finances. If they go undetected, then, in quick time they begin to rein in the movement, holding it captive, in a stranglehold grip that brings slow, painful death.

It is absolutely important, therefore, that the spirit of discernment be active in every ministry. On the practical side, strict standards must be set and adhered to, governing the acceptance, training, counseling and appointment of new converts and transfers to positions of leadership at any level. It takes time and careful screening, coupled with the anointing, to unmask these agents of the devil.

Note carefully, though, that not everyone who transfers from one assembly to another, during a move of God, is into witchcraft. Of course many people move in rebellion and with ulterior motives. However, in many instances, that transfer is orchestrated by the Holy Spirit, in an effort to expose the transferee to a level of the anointing and the atmosphere that is most conducive to him or her fulfilling destiny.

Allow me to cite a situation, which bears witness to the fact that every assembly needs strong powers of discernment, operating at all times, especially when there is a definable outbreak of anointing fire. I remember when the Lord had me as part of a team of ministers that established a ministry in the early 90's. There was an awesome fire burning in the assembly, which attracted people of all walks of life and from all religious persuasions.

One Sunday morning, we began the worship session and could feel the Lord taking us from glory to glory, as we entered into His presence. Suddenly, there was a distinct drop in the intensity of the worship and the tangible presence of God. At the time, I was playing the keyboards, which gave me a vantage point from which to see the faces of the people. I could see discernible stress as the congregation seemed to be struggling against an unseen force that was trying to short-circuit the worship.

I inquired of the Holy Spirit and he immediately alerted me to the presence of a witch in the congregation. I summoned the head intercessor and had her place the prayer warriors at strategic points in the auditorium. As soon as they were in place, I stopped the worship, mounted the platform and informed the rest of the congregation that a witch was in the auditorium and it was time to evict her. Then, I issued a stern warning to whoever the witch might be. I let her know that we knew that she was in the congregation and that she had one of three choices to make by the time I count to three or I would issue a prophetic edict against her. She must come to the altar and repent, leave the auditorium or stay in her seat and drop dead.

By that time, the entire congregation was interceding at a heightened level of spiritual warfare. I waited a while, but saw no movement. Then, I started the count. I reached to three and had already begun to issue the prophetic edict, when, suddenly, above the sound of the public address system, a voice yelled, "Let me pass! Let me pass! I want to get out of here!" It was that of a woman who was dressed in a funny looking robe, complete with a cord around her waist and a cross hanging from her neck. She raced out of the auditorium, ran down the stairs and up the hill towards the centre of town.

Needless to say, immediately, there was a change in the atmosphere. The worship took off on an upward spiral that took us before the throne of God. It was so intense that we could not even minister the word that had been prepared. We always shudder to think what might have happened that day, if the spirit of discernment was not active and that witch was allowed to stay in the house, undetected.

Sectarianism

Apostle Paul had to deal with this spirit in the Church at Corinth, when it was at the height of the move of God that ushered it into existence. He addressed the matter in the first two chapters of the first epistle to the Corinthians.

News had reached Apostle Paul that the congregation had become hotly divided along party lines. Four distinct groupings were identified:

> 1 Corinthians 1:12 TLB: - Some of you are saying, "I am a follower of Paul"; and others say that they are for Apollo's or for Peter; and some that they alone are the true followers of Christ.

By then, the situation had become quite volatile with envy, strife and division, threatening to quench the flames of glory fire in the church. Paul immediately recognized the work of the spirit of sectarian ism and pulled no punches in dealing with it:

> I Corinthians 1:11&13, ASV: 11. For some of those who live at Chloe's house have told me of your arguments and quarrels, dear brothers. 13. Is Christ divided? Was Paul crucified for you? Or were ye baptized into the name of Paul?

Paul followed up this sound rebuke by emphatically laying down the ground rules on how to recognize, appreciate and reckon the corporate effort that goes into birthing, maintaining and retaining the outbreak of anointing fire in any church and in every era. He let the Church at Corinth and, by extension, us today, know that on the first level, the outbreak of anointing fire is both the prerogative and the work of God and not of man.

Yet, on the second level, it is teamwork between God and man; with God as Captain and Director of Operations and us as team members, complementing one another's efforts. Here is how he summed it up in 1 Corinthians 3:3-9, TLB, {It is a bit lengthy, yet, it is a must read for clarity of understanding.}

> ...When you are jealous of one another and divide up into quarreling groups, doesn't that prove you are still babies, wanting your own way? In fact, you are acting like people who don't belong to the Lord at all. 4.
>
> There you are, quarreling about whether I am greater than Apollo's, and dividing the church. Doesn't this show how little you have grown in the Lord? 5. Who am I, and who is Apollo's, that we should be the cause of a quarrel? Why, we're just God's servants, each of us with certain special abilities, and with our help you believed. 6. My work was to plant the seed in your hearts, and Apollo's work was to water it, but it was God, not we, who made

the garden grow in your hearts. 7. The person who does the planting or watering isn't very important, but God is important because he is the one who makes things grow. 8. Apollo's and I are working as a team, with the same aim, though each of us will be rewarded for his own hard work. 9. We are only God's coworkers. You are God's garden, not ours; you are God's building, not ours.

Were these problems exclusive to the Corinthian Church and the era in which it existed? Unfortunately, they were not! From what I have been reading, it seems as though every time glory fires break out, Sectarianism is right there to bring division.

When the great Azusa Street Revival broke out in 1906, everyone- black and white, male and female, rich and poor, fundamentalist and liberal—was together, in one accord, in one place. For as long as it remained like that, anointing fire blazed like an inferno with great signs and wonders. Thousands of people experienced the joys of salvation as they came in droves from across the USA and from around the world, to bask in the glory of God. Then, Sectarianism struck a deadly blow.

After about three and a half years of powerful manifestations of the presence and power of God and harmonious teamwork among the main players in leadership, the eyes of the people were suddenly 'opened'. It dawned on the whites that the overall leader, William Seymour, was black. For them, being led by a black man was an untenable situation. It dawned on the rich and educated that Bro. Seymour was poor and uneducated and, as such, they could no longer accede to his leadership. The blacks, in the movement, suddenly began to be suspicious of the whites and sought to go in their own direction.

Sectarianism pushed each group into taking steps to redress what it thought was a disadvantage against it. The whites, from the USA, broke away and formed the Assemblies of God. Those from Canada formed the Pentecostal Assemblies of Canada. The blacks formed the Church of God In Christ. One hundred years later, division is still taking place within all these groups. Needless to say, the result of this was that the move of God came to a sudden, screeching, gut-wrenching halt.

Is this a call for everyone to remain in one place, when a move of God ignites? Certainly not! The truth is that the place where the anointing is flowing should become a training centre, a filling station and the staging area from which people are sent forth, with apostolic authority and prophetic power, to expand the Kingdom of God, through winning souls, planting churches and establishing support ministries. Jesus himself laid down this sequence of activities as the ground rule for dealing with the outbreak of Holy Ghost fire that birthed the Church in the Upper Room. Even before it broke out, he informed and instructed his disciples, in Acts 1:8,

Acts 1:8,NIV:

But you will receive power when the Holy Spirit comes on you; and you will be my wit nesses in Jerusalem, and in all Judea and Samaria, and to the ends of the earth.

Jesus was really advocating here, that the leaders of a move of God must set plans in place to spread the fire beyond the locale at which the outbreak is happening. The Holy Spirit is the one who will instruct as to when this division for multiplication should take place. When he does, leaders must not let sentimentality or insularity blind them into wanting things to remain as they are. To resist the wooing of the Holy Spirit is to open the door for Sectarianism to move in and engineer splits that will spell death for the move of God.

Here is a governing principle that worked for us, when the anointing fire reached breaking point at the first location where we started ministry. It has served not only to prolong the life of the initial fire at the original place, but also, to spread it to other places in the nation and across the earth, for the last fifteen years. I recommend that the leaders of every move of God should adopt it, if they are to withstand the relentless attacks that the Spirit of Sectarianism will stage against it. One day the Lord said to me, "The anointing in the ministry has reached its critical mass—the point at which many ministries have disintegrated. It is time to divide to multiply or split and die." That we have done and the rest is making history.

Mammon and Greed

Whenever there is a genuine move of God among a people, every facet of life gets touched. Not the least of these is the finances. There is a marked increase from several sources.

On the one hand, the people within the congregation respond to the release of God's love upon them by giving larger offerings more freely. On the other hand, the inevitable increase in the size of the congregation creates a wider financial base and, consequently, a larger intake. Additionally, many who may not even be Christians but who experience healing and deliverance, while attending the services, give lump sum offerings in gratitude to God. Here is where greed and mammon step in and try to hold court.

This psychotic duo banks on leadership not having a properly constituted system of accountability or a premium on financial integrity. If conditions are favorable, they can wreak havoc by engineering embezzlement of funds, exploitation of people's benevolence through spurious promises and attaching dollar value to prophetic utterances. Without fail this will lead to the death of any movement.

Even while writing this book I have become privy to disturbing information, concerning misappropriation of finances, in a ministry, which, up to two years ago, was in the grips of a powerful move of God. Two of the main leaders were the ones who put out the bulk of the initial funds for launching the ministry. All went well until one of them recognized that the equity value on the property had skyrocketed over the years. Overcome by greed and the love of mammon, she decided to cash in.

Unknown to her partner, the rest of the leadership and the congregation, this goodly pastor arranged with a real estate agent to find a buyer for the property. Without paying off the balance remaining on the mortgage transaction, she pocketed the money and sank most of it into the purchase of a luxury home and other items in another city. Then, she suddenly resigned from the church and started another assembly a few miles away from the original address. What was so deceptive and painful was the fact that she allowed her partner to carry on service as usual in the building, without any indication of the under handed action that she had taken. It was only some time later, when the new owners came to take pos session of the property that her former partner knew that the building had been sold.

When last I heard of the situation, litigation had begun against the pastor to recover the money, which she had realized from the transaction. Additionally, and sadly so, the ministry that she had started was no more in operation. It continues to beat me how per sons, in such situations, can ever expect their efforts to succeed.

The original congregation has had to relocate at least three times in the last eighteen months in an effort to find a place that is affordable as far as rent is concerned. The numbers have dwindled and many who have remained are reluctant to put their all into ministry because of the fear of such a scenario playing out itself again. Some have backslidden and want to hear nothing about church anymore. Such is the devastating power of mammon and greed.

Knowing that a genuine move of God precipitates increase at all levels, including finances, it behooves all leaders to set proper accounting procedures in place, even while the intake is still small. No one person, not even the maximum leader, should be able to spend cash beyond a certain ceiling or use checks without a second signature on a voucher or check. Neither should acquisition or disposal of property be effected with only a single signature. The counting and banking of money should be put in the hands of a team of honest, trustworthy people who have a healthy fear for God and the ministry at heart. No single individual should be allowed to make the final tally away from the watchful eyes of the rest of the team.

I know of a large ministry in Trinidad that was swindled of over $500,000 by the head elder. The practice of the finance committee was to do the counting of the money as a team. However, they would leave the final tallying and the making of the bank deposits in the hands of the head elder. Without any prior notice, one day, the said elder informed the pastor that he was migrating to a metropolitan country by the next morning.

At the next meeting of the elders, the pastor called for a financial report. When the internal records were compared with the returns from the bank, it was discovered that there was a discrepancy to the tune of over $500,000 between the two records. It was only then that it became clear that, for a period of over fifteen years, the head elder would siphon some of the funds into his personal account, every time he made a deposit. He managed to keep it under wraps because, since it was he who received the monthly bank returns, he was able to conceal them from both the pastor and the rest of the finance committee. By the time his wrong doing was discovered, the head elder was well on his way to his new life, far from the reach of the pastor.

Very lamentably, though, the pastor refused to put the matter in the hands of the police because he wanted to avoid a scandal. Well, the scandal still broke out anyway and what was funny is that all the blame was thrown squarely on the shoulders of the pastor.

Of course, we are not naïve to think that Greed and Mammon will not eventually find a way around the tightest system. However, as long as there is one in place and it is regularly reviewed, it will help to save the ministry and leadership from embarrassment and headache. It will also help to keep some people out of jail. Our goodly pastor should have been more vigilant.

Sins of the Flesh

Many moves of God have been derailed because the spirit of immorality camouflages itself with the general air of liberty that pervades the atmosphere in the congregation. Under the cover of hugging and kissing and openness of relationships, he creeps in and entraps those who have not yielded their members to God, in a spiral of illicit, clandestine sexual relationships. He then sets things up so that maxi mum exposure will take place. As soon as such news hit both the airwaves and the 'ear waves' things inevitably fall apart, especially when key leaders are involved. BEWARE!

Sins of the Flesh play for big stakes. It has felled many a leader who had been running well and who, as it were, had begun to smell the fragrance of the throne room of God—so deep had he been immersed in the fires of sacrificial praise and Spirit-led worship. This spirit has the unique ability to mutate into countless subtle, deceptive variations. Chief among them are adultery, fornication, immoral thoughts, homosexuality, pornography and incest.

In the height of his success, King David was viciously attacked by Sins of the Flesh, as he walked upon the rooftop of his palace one day. Idleness had set him up for this attack. He was supposed to have been out leading his troops in battle, but had chosen to send others to do the job, while he stayed at home to 'chill out'. In his pursuit of leisure, he allowed the pleasure of sin to dominate him, sending for and proceeding to commit adultery with Bathsheba, the woman he saw bathing herself, while he walked on his rooftop.

The narrative in 2 Samuel u is more intriguing than any of the modern day soap operas. It traces the stages through which idleness led David into lust; lust led to adultery; adultery led to deception; deception led to murder; murder led to hardness of heart and lying. All of this led to the exposure of David by God through Nathan, the prophet.

In Psalms 51, David aptly portrays the level of devastation that this thief inflicts, when he sinks his evil, poisonous fangs into one's spirit. Lying prostrate upon God's mercy seat, David cries out for the restoration of the joy of salvation, which has been so cruelly snatched from him. The trauma leads him to ask for a washing, cleaning and purging of his soul and the installation of a new heart within him by God.

The Apostle Paul recognized the great potential of Sins of the Flesh to wreak havoc on the child of God and on the moves of God in His Church. Consequently, he dedicated huge chunks of his writings to presenting the antidote against it. His resolution was that we should roast our flesh upon the fire of God's altar, as the only safe way of avoiding defeat by Sins of the Flesh: "I beseech you therefore, brethren...that you present your bodies a living sacrifice, holy, acceptable unto God." (Romans 12:1).

The rationale here is that drastic situations call for drastic measures.

Paul waxes even more macabre in writing to the Colossians. In Colossians 3:5, he declares, "Mortify (kill), therefore, your members which are upon the earth..." Verse 9 further admonishes "...put off (banish) the old man with his deeds." Then he clinches the entire prescription with the positive instruction of verse 1o, "...put on the new man which is renewed in knowledge, after the image of him that created him." All of us, caught in the midst of anointing fire, at present, or are eagerly seeking God for such, should take heed!

Strange Fire

The fire, upon the brazen altar in the tabernacle in the wilderness, was a type of the true revival fire, which the Lord wants to ignite among his people in this season, both in its origin and in the requirements for its maintenance and application.

The origin of this fire was definitely divine, having come directly out of the presence of the Lord (Leviticus 9:24). The original fuel upon which it fed was the animal sacrifices of the people mingled with portions of special incense selected under divine direction. This combination of sacrifice and incense burning in the fire produced a sweet smelling savor that ascended as a smoke unto the Lord. Out of this fire upon the altar, the priests and Levites would take lighted coals, which were placed with incense inside a censor and waved regularly before the altar, as a tribute of praise and thanksgiving unto the Lord.

This act was the earthly reenactment of what John saw much later in Heaven, as recorded in Revelation 8. In that scene, John saw the Lord give incense to a strong angel who put it in a golden censor together with fire from the altar, which burned continuously before the Lord's throne. The smoke from the censor ascended up before the Lord as a sweet odor.

In essence, the fire upon the altar in the tabernacle also had to be kept alight continuously, so that there would be a perpetual source of lighted coals for the censor that the priests used. To ensure that this was so, Moses appointed two of Aaron's sons, Nadab and Abihu, to be the keepers of the flame and to wave the censors of burning incense unto the Lord.

According to Leviticus 10:1&2, it would seem that Nadab and Abihu either became complacent with their calling or had been distracted by some form of enticement. Whatever the cause, though, it is clear that the fire went out. Naturally, they found themselves in a serious predicament, when it came time for the waving of the censor of incense: there was no fire upon the altar with which to light the censor. What did they do?

Nadab and Abihu ought to have gone to Uncle Moses and Daddy Aaron to inform them of the situation, so that they could have obtained fresh fire from the Lord. Instead, they presumed that any old fire would do and promptly proceeded to use fire from another source. The Amplified Bible labels it as 'strange and unholy fire.' (Leviticus 10:1). God's response was swift and decisive- "And there came forth fire from the Lord, and devoured them and they died before the Lord." (Leviticus 10:2).

Aaron was taken aback by the swiftness and severity of God's judgment upon his sons. He apparently looked to Moses for an explanation. God's wisdom filled Moses and He had him say unto Aaron, "I (and my will, not their own) will be acknowledged as hallowed by those who come near me, and before all the people I will be honored." (Leviticus 10:3, AMP).

As it turns out, this was not simply a word aimed at placating Aaron's grief, but rather a valuable teaching tool for the Church today, as we enter a season of unprecedented manifestations of the presence of God. Here are some of the lessons it teaches:

- When God lights His fire among His people,

  He holds them responsible for providing the fuel that will keep it burning.

- Give God the glory that is due to Him. Anything else could spell disaster.
- God's will is paramount and He is still disposed to judge those who would violate it.
- If any man lacks fire or if what he has goes out, let him asks God for fresh fire. Never light your own.
- To offer strange fire to God is to sign one's own death warrant, sometimes physically but definitely spiritually.

Seducing Spirits

It seems as though a move of God always succeeds in attracting a profusion of what can only be termed as Seducing Spirits. Their line of attack is to apply to the present move of God the same kind of pressure that they did, when they first appeared in scripture. In pursuit of this, they seek to recruit human agents to do their dirty work. Not surprisingly, there is apparently no end of volunteers for the task. Of course, their expressed aim is to kill the move of God.

Here is a short list of some of these spirits. Their identities are derived from the main players in the episode in which they first appeared in scripture. Bear in mind, though, that this list is but a sample of the myriad of seducing spirits that attacked moves of God in Bible times:

- *The Jezebel Spirit whose area of specialization is to take control of proceedings, by seeking to kill the leader of the move of God. (1 Kings 19).*

- *The Korah Spirit, which spawns rebellion against designated leadership. (Numbers 16).*

- *The Absolom Spirit, which seeks promotion by attracting unto himself the attention and allegiance of others away from divinely anointed and appointed leadership. (2 Samuel 15-19).*

- *The Delilah Spirit whose specialty is to seduce leadership into committing acts of immorality. In this way it short-circuits their anointing and renders them powerless by robbing them of vision, integrity and strength. (Judges 16).*

- *The Ananias and Saphira Spirit, which tries to gain mileage by creating impressions. (Acts 5).*

- *The Judas Spirit, which has betrayal of leadership on its mind. (Matthew 26& 27).*

A most important point to consider, here, is that these principalities have the uncanny ability of mutating into a form peculiar to the nature of the move of God, in a particular place and time. That is all the more reason why it behooves all who desire to or may be already experiencing a move of God to set a watch against these agents of death. Peter's admonition in 1 Peter 5:8&9, TLB, is very instructional in establishing the appropriate level of preparedness.

> Be careful-watch out for attacks from Satan, your great enemy. He prowls around like a hungry, roaring lion, looking for some victim to tear apart. (9). Stand firm when he attacks. Trust the Lord; and remember that other Christians all around the world are going through these sufferings too.

Religion vs. Revelation

It is an irrefutable truth that the spark, which finally sets off the flames of anointing fire, comes via a fresh revelation of truth. This may take place by way of a direct prophecy, prophetic preaching, a vision, a dream or a still small voice, depositing the mind of God into the spirit of the leader. Based on the principle of maintenance, which we explored previously, it means, then, that for this fire to continue to burn and expand, it must continue to be fuelled by revelation. But alas, therein lies the problem.

At some point, soon after the fire ignites, a wicked spirit called Religion begins to spin its flame quenching web. He targets someone within the leadership or someone who may have influence with them, in whom he plants a seed of stagnation. He does this by creating an illusion that the new revelation is or will soon come under attack. Then, he presents to this leader a simple plan for guarding the new move of God against such an eventuality. On the surface, this may sound very noble, but at its deeper level, it brings slow, painful death to the move of God. Here is how it works.

Immediately upon receipt of the initial spark that ignites into a fire, Religion dupes leadership into thinking that the present revelation is the final item that God has in His treasury of truths. Such thinking sends leadership into preservation mode. What happens next is similar, in principle, to steps taken in a fertility lab to store sperms for later use. The major difference, though, is that, whereas in the lab such action gives life, as far as a move of God is concerned, it brings death.

As soon as the lab technician takes possession of the sperms from the donor, he quick freezes them in a solution of liquid nitrogen, which carries one of the lowest sub-zero temperatures. The reason for such quick action is so that the quality of the sperms will not be compromised, greatly enhancing the possibility of conception, for the woman into whom they are implanted, at a later date.

In similar vein, Religion cons leadership into quick freezing the revelation, hoping to preserve it for all times. It does so by making it its major and, sometimes, it's only point of reference for the weaving of an intricate mix of doctrines, dogmas and rituals. This action effectively creates an environment of traditions, so tight and unyielding, that nothing new stands the light of day for consideration, let alone incorporation.

While all of this is happening, the brightness of the initial flames continues to attract people by the masses to the meeting place with little effort on the part of the leaders. This convinces leadership that they have applied the correct measures. Later on, though, as the flames inevitably begin to die due to lack of the fuel that fresh revelation brings, they are forced to implement different strategies in an effort to continue attracting people. Some such strategies include free meals after services and the promise of posting to high positions for new recruits.

Regardless of the stage at which they come in, though, recruits are trained in the art of blowing the cold, arctic air of blind loyalty and unquestioning commitment towards the original revelation, which began red hot, but which now rests at the core of a block of stone-cold, unfeeling legalism. It is then one starts hearing expressions from the lips of leadership such as:

- 'This is the only ministry that preaches the gospel as Jesus did.'
- 'No one must attend services in any other ministry. Anyone found doing so will be dealt with severely. 'We cannot guarantee your protection from transference of spirits in those other places.
- 'A curse will come upon anyone who leaves this ministry.'
- 'Whatever God has to say, in this ministry, He must say it through me. I am the leader, here!'
- "This is my ministry and I will guard it with my life.
- These are my ushers and my elders and my choir and my members. Nobody gets them to do anything without my permission.'

At first, these statements cause trumpets to blast and bells to ring warning signals of impending danger, within the mind of the spiritually sensitive individual. However, he readily dismisses them as being either his own imagination or lies from the devil. You see, religion has used sentimentality, blind loyalty and intimidation to condition him into accepting the infallibility of his leader. Added to this, is the power that such a leader exerts. This power is always commensurate with his charismatic personality and his stature, which draws on the size and popularity of the move of God over which he presides.

However, the trouble begins, when this individual begins looking at other ministers on television or accepts invitations to attend conferences in other assemblies. In those settings, he becomes exposed to another view on the same revelation, which he has been helping to keep frozen. He also hears fresh new truths that God has been releasing. He returns to the assembly and resumes his position and assignment. The only problem, though, is that the freshness of the new revelation, which is now flowing within him and the passion for answers to the questions that have popped up since being exposed to new truths, are now causing a major thaw in the corner of the ice block where he is blowing.

This infraction does not go unnoticed by the relevant authorities. Their response is swift and ruthless. They immediately activate their damage control machinery. Without providing any room for redress, they take steps to put the individual out of the ministry, labeling him as a heretic, a rebel and a danger to the cause. For insurance, they may even round up all those to whom he may have spoken. They issue strong threats to them and, sometimes, to the rest of the congregation about them suffering a similar fate, if they persist in asking certain questions or continues to embrace the new truths, in question.

What such leaders fail to recognize is the fact that, by adopting such a position, they willingly become agents of Religion to unwittingly actualize one of the saddest truths of history, which states: The most vocal and vicious attacks against a new move of God are launched, more often than not, by leaders who have made a religion out of the previous move. Such is the power of Religion.

It was Religion that attacked Peter on the mountain, when Jesus became transfigured in Matthew 17. Upon seeing the spectacle of Jesus shining like the noonday sun and Moses and Elijah speaking with him, Peter blurted out,

> *...Lord, it is good for us to be here: if thou wilt, let us make here three tabernacles; one for thee, and one for Moses, and one for Elias (Matthew 17:4).*

Peter intended to do exactly what we have been describing in this section, so far. He wanted to quick freeze the experience by building three tabernacles, one each for Jesus, Moses and Elijah. On the surface, that sounded all well and good. However, God saw motive above structure. He knew that if He allowed Peter to follow through on his plan, Peter would form three denominations, built according to man's ordinance and pattern and contrary to God's master plan. Such a move would completely preempt God's own ability to keep bringing Peter and the rest of us, by extension, into new, life-changing, spiritual experiences. Consequently, even before Peter's words could fully leave his mouth and become established as seed, in the atmosphere, God boomed from the Heavens with emphatic authority,

> ... *This is my beloved Son, in whom I am well pleased; hear ye him. (Matthew 17:5, KJV).*

God was warning all and sundry that, when He initiates a new move in the earth, He would rather us work with Him, instead of us setting out our own plans and then inviting Him to work with us. He was making it clear that He was a dynamic God, full of new things that He is willing to impart to us and not the proverbial 'one trick pony' that religion tries to make Him out to be. Hence the reason for God's admonition to Peter that he should shut up and desist from issuing instructions to Jesus. Rather, he should open his ear to hear what Jesus had to say for that moment and always.

We must take cognizance of the admonition in Deuteronomy 8:3, NIV, "...man does not live on bread alone but on every word that comes from the mouth of the Lord." God is always declaring new things. It is our responsibility, therefore, to position ourselves in a place where God is speaking and be willing to obey what He says. Our personal lives, that of the ministry and that of the fire of God in any given sea son, depend on us continuing to do so.

Here is a short list of the negative fallout that occurs when Religion is allowed to attack a move of God unchallenged:

- Leaders lose their passion to move on to new experiences in God.
- People are willing to defend what God has said, but refuse to accept what God is saying, now.
- Religion dupes a leader into taking off the wheels of his wagon, placing the wagon on blocks, while still accelerating the engine at full throttle using up a lot of energy, but going nowhere.
- Leaders follow a policy of exclusion, which creates stagnation and ultimately leads to a quenching of the fire.

Herein, then, lies the counter measure to the master spirit called Religion: an ear that continues to hear what the Spirit has to say to the Church and a heart that is covenanted to carrying out the instructions. Do this and a spark will ignite into a fire and the fire will blaze into a raging inferno that will continue to burn perpetually. It may undergo several permutations, but it will never go out.

Egotism

Having been raised in Church as a pastor's son, I have not only been eye witness to several mighty moves of God, but have also been personally involved in several of them over the years. Sadly, though, I have also seen many of them that once swept everything before them, fizz out into nothingness, at worst, or become a hollow sounding shell, at best, under the relentless attack from enemy forces. In addition to those forces already identified and profiled above, Egotism has proven to be one of the most destructive flame quenchers of them all.

Egotism is another word for pride. It fills a leader with such a feeling of self importance that he begins to believe that he has become the centre of the universe. He sees himself as the sole bearer and custodian of the anointing. As such, he arranges the affairs of the ministry so that, as long as he is not present, nothing significant can take place. In fact, he would institute policy that actually attempts to predetermine what types of manifestations of the Holy Spirit, if any at all, are allowed in his absence.

Now, I am well aware of the fact that God usually operates through a set man or woman, in any given arena where glory fire is raging. Neither am I naïve to the fact that almost inevitably, have people tended to equate the progress of the move of God with that individual. However, the problem arises, when that set man/woman loses sight of the fact that he or she is simply: (1). a vessel into whom God has chosen to pour His Spirit, (2). a channel through which God is trying to get His Spirit to flow to others. (3). the lead sheep that carries the bell around its neck to direct others to God, the source of the anointing.

A set man/woman should know that, although the anointing is absolutely pure, at its source, which is the heart of God, it can become contaminated, if, at the time of entry into his/her inner man, there are traces of pride and other such impurities. He/she must also know that pride is a channel blocker that chokes the free flow of the anointing from him/her to others. Additionally, as the lead sheep, the pride, in his/her heart, may cause him/her to lead God's people to draw from a source that is laced with tainted scriptural interpretations and twisted spiritual practices, rendering them tainted and contaminated, as well.

In such a scenario, God is left with no choice but to cut off the flow of His Spirit, at its source, until the set man cleans out his vessel, so as to present Him with a sterilized environment for the anointing and a debris-free conduit for getting it to others. If that is too long in coming, God eventually bypasses the set man by taking the bell from around his neck and placing it on that of another of His choosing.

You may be wondering why God will do such a thing. I am so glad you asked! You see, God is always driven by a desire to get His anointing to His people for a particular season more than He is given to promoting any single individual. Consequently, if after repeatedly presenting opportunities for change. There is none on the part of the leader, He cuts him off. Therefore, when God elects a man as the set man to lead His people in a particular season, that man should count it as a special privilege and not see it as some divine right of his. As such, he must behave himself circumspectly.

Of course, one does not always see the effect of this cutting off, right away. Sometimes, it takes many years before complete shutdown takes place. Often, this makes the perpetrator think that all is well because he still sees the hand of God moving mightily, when he ministers. As such, in spite of the myriad of prophetic warnings that may come, he sees no need to amend his ways. Little does he know, though, that he is running on residual power and the sheer grace of God. Realistically, nothing new is happening. He is just depressing the rewind button, every time he stands to minister. However, he is heading for an inevitable meltdown. It is like unplugging a fan. For a few seconds, the blade keeps spinning, with little evidence that disconnection has occurred. However, with time, starved of a free flow of current, operations grind to a definitive halt. A strong case in point is what happened with King Saul, as recorded in 1 Samuel 13.

Sometime, within the 20th year of his reign, as king over Israel, Saul took it upon himself to offer a burnt offering unto God-a function reserved for Samuel, the prophet (1 Samuel 13). He had mustered a rag tag band of men in an effort to shake off the oppression of the Philistines from Israel. He had also agreed to wait seven days before launching any offensive, so that Samuel could come to offer sacrifice unto the Lord, which would have guaranteed victory over the enemy. However, in the face of overwhelming odds and with his army fragmenting before his eyes, Saul decided that it was time to take action. Impatience and impetuousness drove him to presume that, in the face of his problems and in the light of Samuel being long in coming, he could take action outside of his jurisdiction. As fate would have it, as soon as he was finished with the sacrifice, Samuel arrived.

On Samuel's arrival, Saul went out to meet him with all the customary salutations. However, Samuel was not impressed. Indignant about what Saul had done, Samuel asked him for an explanation. It is in Saul's reply that we see the extent to which egotism had infected him:

> *Saul replied, "I saw my men scattering from me, and you didn't arrive when you said you would, and the Philistines are at Micmash ready for battle. 12. So I said, 'The Philistines are ready to march against us, and I haven't even asked for the LORD'S help!' So I felt obliged to offer the burnt offering myself before you came." (1 Samuel 13:11–12, NLT).*

Notice that in just these two short verses Saul managed to use the personal pronoun 'I' and its derivatives on at least seven occasions. This is a tell tale sign of the Egotism Syndrome (E.S.). When E.S. strikes, it is no longer what God says or wants, as it was at the onset of the move of God. The leader now thinks that he has a handle on God. Consequently, he does things from his own human perspective, expecting God to come and endorse his actions. It is no longer God's work or God's people. The leader sees it as his ministry, his men, his elders and his ushers and so forth. An attitude of this nature only serves to kindle the wrath of God and leads Him to look for another lead sheep, around whose neck to put the bell. This was exactly what He did, in the case of Saul.

Upon hearing Saul's excuse, Samuel, acting on God's behalf, delivered the following indictment and judgment against Saul:

> *"You acted foolishly," Samuel said. "You have not kept the command the LORD your God gave you; if you had, he would have established your Kingdom over Israel for all time. 14 But now your Kingdom will not endure; the Lord has sought out a man after his own heart and appointed him leader of his people, because you have not kept the Lord's command." (1 Samuel 13:13-14, NIV).*

It is important to note, though, that it was not until 1 Samuel 31, we read of Saul's reign coming to a horrendous end. Wounded in his final battle with the Philistines, he committed suicide by falling on his sword. His death made way for David, God's choice for king, to take ruler ship. This was some twenty years after the indictment and judgment were delivered by Samuel. He continued to reign on residual power for all these years, until the inevitable shutdown came.

During those years, Saul showed proof of the dangers of running on residual power and sheer grace. He continued to disobey God's instructions by doing things his way. He became vindictive to the point of attempting to eliminate his competition, David, through at least twenty-one failed assassination attempts. When Samuel died, Saul realized that he was truly cut off from God, but instead of retuning his spirit to God's frequency, by way of repentance; he indulged himself in witchcraft, one of the things that God hates with a passion. This seemed to have been the last straw. It caused God to turn his face from Saul, leaving him to the mercies of the enemy who destroyed him.

What drastic action on God's part! What a devastating end for a man who was anointed to take Israel into a new season! What a serious warning for all those upon whom God has placed the divine responsibility of being keepers of the flames of His anointing!

Lest there is someone reading this who would practice egotism and think that he would get as wide a window as Saul's in which to operate, it is my solemn duty to admonish you that there are also times when God issues an indictment and executes judgment all in one motion, thus leaving no window for repentance. Follow the story of:

- Uzziah, in 2 Kings 14 & 2 Chronicles 26. During his reign, as king over Judah, Uzziah triggered a virtual national revival: the economy prospered, the army became invincible, using new weapons of war which he had invented, to crush his enemies and Jerusalem was fortified, like never before. However, one day success got to his head. He entered the temple and, in defiance of the admonition of the priests, attempted to burn incense before the Lord. In 2 Kings 15:5, we are merely told that "The Lord smote the king, so that he was a leper unto the day of his death..." No window for repentance!
- Nebuchadnezzar, king of Babylon, in Daniel 4: God had blessed him with wisdom and might, such that he became ruler of the entire then known world. He instituted many

policies and completed major projects that made Babylon a veritable star city and the headquarters of his operations. One day, when he had completed his pet project, the hanging gardens (which have been immortalized in history as one of the seven wonders of the world), he strutted along the balcony of his palace, beheld his handiwork and said, "Is not this the great Babylon I have built as the royal residence, by my mighty power and for the glory of my majesty?" (Daniel 4:30, NIV). Daniel records that, "The words were still on his lips when a voice came from heaven, "This is what is decreed for you, King Nebuchadnezzar: Your royal authority has been taken from you. You will be driven away from people and will live with the wild animals; you will eat grass like cattle. Seven times will pass by for you until you acknowledge that the Most High is sovereign over the Kingdoms of men and gives them to anyone he wishes." (Daniel 4:31&32, NIV). Indictment and execution came in one breath!

- Ananias and Saphira, in Acts 5: Like so many others, caught up in the new move of God at Jerusalem, they sold property and brought the money and laid it at the feet of the apostles. However, their motives were wrong. Theirs was not an act of benevolence. Rather, it was an attempt to gain some attention for themselves and make an impression upon the apostles and the congregation. Apostle Peter saw through their lie and instead of pronouncing upon them the blessings that come with such acts of benevolence, he passed a death sentence upon them. They both died, right at the apostle's feet. They had no window for repentance.

Tourist Attraction

Fire naturally attracts people. No one has to send for them. They are simply drawn by the phenomenon of a fire raging through a building or forest. The problem, though, is that many of them come as mere spectators and make no contribution to the improvement of the situation at hand. In fact, many of them get in the way of the bona fide firemen, who are there to perform their duty of extinguishing the fire. It is no wonder, then, that on such occasions the police put up barriers to keep the crowd at bay.

It is much the same in the Spirit. Wherever the fire of God has broken out in any significant way, over the years, one thing that has inevitably happened is that throngs of people have shown up. It happened in Judah, as recorded in 2 Chronicles 15. When King Asa deconsecrated himself and encouraged the people to wholly obey the Lord, Judah began to prosper. As a consequence, people from the other tribes of Israel migrated to Judah in abundance. It was the same, on the day of Pentecost, when Holy Ghost fire broke out in the Upper Room. Multitudes gathered to witness the spectacle and, on that very day, the congregation grew from 120 to 3,120 worshippers (Acts 2).

The very thing happened again in one of the most widely publicized moves of God, in recent times, which commentators dubbed 'The Brownsville Revival', in Pensacola, Florida. Over the six years, 1995 to 2001, during which it was at its peak, it was reported that millions of people came from all around the world to witness the happenings in the assembly. Be it known, though, that all did not have the same agenda.

As news about the manifestation of the power of God spread, some people came to the meetings with a genuine hunger for God. Those were the ones who invariably (1) experienced the joy of salvation, even to the tune of over 100,000, within the first three years, according to the records, (2) renewed their faith in God, after years of backsliding and (3) became activated in the gifts of the Spirit. Many of the ministers of the gospel who attended went back to their home churches, in far flung areas of the earth, with an impartation of the anointing so strong that the fire of the Lord broke out in their respective locales, as well.

There were also those who came as spectators, just to see what was going on. To them, the manifestations of the Spirit of God held nothing but entertainment value similar to what they might have experienced in a circus. In such a case, all that was lost was the fact that they stood in the midst of God's manifested glory and neither recognized nor responded appropriately to it. The fallout on the movement itself was negligible, except for the occupation of a few seats in which others with an inward hunger for God could have sat and gleaned something beneficial.

However, it is the following categories of attendees, which in my estimation, did more evil than good for the move at Brownsville. It serves as a warning for the rest of the Church, as people seek God for the outbreak of Holy Ghost fire, in their midst, in this and in seasons to come.

There were those ministers who visited the Brownsville Assembly as mimics. Their aim was to see how they could decipher a method by which things were being done, copy it and return home with a view of duplicating it in their respective ministries. Many of them did manage to experience some degree of manifestation on their return home.

However, because it was not a genuine transformation of spirit and mindset, which only comes by way of a personal encounter with God, it soon fizzled and things returned to business as usual.

I distinctly remember this happening to quite a few ministers from Trinidad and Tobago, my native country. Many of them were steeped in tradition but took the step to visit the Brownsville Assembly anyway, since it was the fashionable thing to do at the time. Upon their return, there were the undeniable signs of prophesying, falling out in the spirit while preaching, the use of expressions such as "God is doing a new thing" and that general uplift in the atmosphere of their respective congregations.

In fact, one did not even have to have known that a particular pastor had made the trip—the signs spoke for themselves. The common question was "What happened to Pastor X? How come he is dancing and prophesying like that? This is totally out of character for him!" The usual answer would be, 'He went to Brownsville, Pensacola.

Needless to say, though, after a few weeks, the sizzling fire fizzled into nothingness. Like poison ivy slowly creeping over a recently painted wall, the spirit of tradition rebounded to reclaim its ascendancy over proceedings, because there was no internal transformation.

Then, there were those who went to Brownsville simply as skeptics, critics and fault finders. Their expressed aim was to scrutinize everything for anything negative, be it sermon or prophecy, altar call or financial appeal, dance or fallout under the anointing. Among them were journalists, talk show hosts, writers and, sadly, ministers of the gospel. They turned the front row seats of the auditorium into the seats of the scornful. They recorded their findings for the sole purpose of mounting a campaign of negative publicity against the move of God. You just have to do a search of the World Wide Web for sites pertaining to the Brownsville Revival and it will appall you to see the scores of articles, critical of almost every aspect of the move at Brownsville, penned by fellow ministers of the gospel and editors of both secular and Christian-based publications.

Before I am accused of nitpicking, let me put the actions of the mimics and the critics in perspective, as it relates to the demise of not only the Brownsville Revival, but also, of every move of God, into which they are allowed to sink their poisonous fangs, undetected and unrestrained. When the mimics show up, they add nothing to the proceedings. Instead, they come in the spirit of the leech, which is a sucker that gorges itself on the blood of its victim, until it has had its fill. Its victim is left all the worse for wear because the blood that it has just lost represents its very life. It is much the same with a move of God, when mimics are around. Each of them gorges himself on the anointing, which is the fuel that feeds the fire. They are nothing but anointing suckers, for want of a better term. Over a period of time, their cumulative sucking action exerts enough pressure upon the fuel system to threaten the longevity of the move of God.

The mimics also come in the spirit of the viper, using a million different disguises; in the spirit of the wolf, having an insatiable appetite for ripping fresh meat (unsuspecting leadership) to shreds and in the spirit of the vulture, with pen (knife) in hand, ready to carve out their pound of flesh. Variations on these personas have already been identified a few paragraphs above. They very stealthily wiggle their way until they are perched in strategic positions from which they can make a deadly strike at their targets, which are mainly:

- Leadership—the ones that give direction to the movement.
- The prophetic anointing—the source of revelation from which the movement receives a fresh supply of nourishment.
- The worship—the source of divine presence, which is the heart and the pulse of the movement.
- The miracles, signs and wonders, which lend authenticity to the movement.

When the critics strike, they inject paralyzing venom, in the form of doubt and skepticism, into the nerve centre of the fire, causing people to question the authenticity of the miracles and prophecies. They attempt to set the movement adrift by ripping the character of key leaders to shreds, in public are such as newspapers, radio, television, magazines and pulpits. It is a case of striking the shepherd so that the sheep will scatter.

Judging from the articles, which they publish, it seems safe to conclude that many of the critics, especially those disguised as ministers of the gospel, are really fuelled by jealousy and anger. When fuelled by jealousy, instead of celebrating with the designated leader, their thinking is 'It should have been me! Since it is not me, I will destroy it.'

Where anger is the driving force, it often stems from the fact that the fresh revelation and prophetic utterances are doing more than just mounting a challenge against long held traditions of men. They are empowering faithful adherents to trade their places in those arenas, for a more meaningful relationship with God, in a different environment in which they can find expression. In an article on the internet pertaining to the Brownsville Revival, a pastor of the same denomination, accused the leadership of the assembly of being responsible for many bright, promising young ministers leaving the denomination to pursue ministerial interests in a different direction.

Many defenders of the old system cannot tolerate such an eventuality and set out to identify weak spots in the new move, which they hope to exploit until it grinds to an agonizing halt. This is their way of avenging the death of their sacred cows and getting back their pound of flesh. What must not go unnoticed is the fact that, when the assembly within which the fire breaks out is part of a larger denomination, as in the case of the Brownsville Revival, the anger and jealousy factors are all too evident, even bordering on appalling.

What is just as dangerous as the attacks themselves is the residual spirits that the attackers leave behind, when they board their means of transportation to return to their homes. They leave the assembly and its environs like a virtual minefield, strewn with unexploded bombs. These explosives are embedded in the minds of people in the form of doubt, suspicion, skepticism, rebellion, fear and disunity. They have been set there by the critics while conducting inter views with members and attendees, using questions that are loaded equally for implanting the spirit of suggestion as they are for gleaning information. All that is needed is for a leader or someone intimately involved in the movement to do or say something that seems questionable and a massive explosion of accusations, rumors, desertions and so on, will be set off, rocking the very foundations of the movement. Such is the danger posed by the critics that, even after they have left, they still have the capability of inflicting untold damage on a move of God.

The questions that naturally arise are 'How does a move of God deal with such a relentless onslaught from these tourists? Can it prevent those attacks, in the first place? Can it survive them at all? If they are inevitable, what measures should be put in place to minimize the negative fallout that they cause?' The following is a shortlist of guidelines, which the Holy Spirit has downloaded to me as counter measures for effectively handling such attacks:

- Leadership must know that attacks on any move of God are inevitable. As such, they should not feel discouraged, wondering why this one is being attacked. Contrary to the critics, it is not a punishment from God for some hidden sin. Remember that every move of God packs enough power to dismantle the strongholds of Satan, not only in the immediate vicinity and season, but also, nationwide and, even, internationally for generations to come. Will Satan sit by idly and do nothing about it? I doubt that very much. He attacked the moves of God in Eden, in the Upper Room, at Azusa Street, in Brownsville and he is going to come after the one in your neck of the woods. So, govern yourself accordingly.

- Leadership must take to heart Gamaliel's advice to the Sanhedrin Counsel in Acts 5:38. He was warning them against trying to quench the fire of God, which had broken out, in the Upper Room, only months before. He warned them, "Leave these men alone! Let them go! For if their purpose or activity is of human origin, it will fail. But if it is from God, you will not be able to stop these men; you will only find yourselves fighting against God." (Acts 5:38&39, NIV). Every leader must know that if the fire is truly from God, no man can put it out. It may undergo several mutations, but it will not go out.
- Every leader must be convinced, in his own heart, that it is God who has appointed and anointed him to lead the present move, lest, under the pressure of relentless attacks, he turns tail and runs.
- Every leader must know that under such powerful light, as the one cast by the intense glory of God, flaws, both personal and corporate, are bound to surface, from time to time. Instead of trying to justify oneself, admit what should be admitted; confess what should be confessed; quit what must be quitted and move on.
- Set watchmen on the walls around the clock. Prophets and intercessors must be persistently vigilant. They must be strategically positioned throughout the congregation, sniffing the air, as it were, for the mimics and the critics. As soon as any untoward situation crops up, they must raise an alarm and activate a prearranged plan of attack to strike it down, before it can cause any damage.
- There must be regular sessions of purging and pruning of the congregation. This principle is based on the practice recommended by manufacturers of both the gas stove and

the oil lamp for maintaining efficiency of operations. They know that, under normal conditions, there is a buildup of carbon on the burners and wicks as fuel is being consumed. If left unattended, this carbon chokes the flow of fuel, greatly inhibiting the ability of the burner to heat the pots and that of the lamp to give light. Consequently, it is the householder's responsibility to do it himself or call in one so skilled to service the burner or trim the wick of the lamp to improve efficiency. It stands to reason, then, that since a move of God is equated with fire, the same action must be taken in principle. Wherever this principle is practiced, the critics will be hard pressed to find, in all honesty, a flaw to exploit legitimately.

- God has vested the responsibility for maintenance of the purity of the move in the hands of the leader. The leader has the authority to rein in any extremity of behavior, by calling on the individuals to cease their practice. Remember that God sends the rain, but it is our responsibility to keep dredging the river bed and raising the river banks, so that the waters do not overflow and devastate the land.
- Not all who come to the meetings are there for the long haul. When the going gets rough and the revelations go deeper, many of the thrill seekers will jump on their surf boards and look for another wave to ride. It happened to Jesus, in John 6:53–59. When he raised the level of his ministry from doing fast food miracles to teaching the deeper things of the Kingdom, many complained, "...these are hard sayings." (John 6:59). From that day, they followed him no more.

Exaggeration

One day, a pastor came to see me for counseling. He was doing quite well, as far as expansion and impact in ministry were concerned. He told of a problem that he was having with exaggeration, which we immediately agreed was lying by another name. He would travel abroad to minister and in his report to the folks back home, he would tell them of the hundreds of people who attended the meetings and received their miracles, although, in actuality, there were not even a hundred people, in any given service He lamented that he had prayed and fasted continually, trying to break the cycle, but to no avail. The guilt, shame and condemnation were becoming too burdensome for him to bear. He needed help and he needed it fast, lest he fell apart.

Immediately, the Lord led me to ask him about his upbringing, as it pertained to his relationship with his father. He seemed startled at my line of questioning and thereupon, he broke into a gut wrenching scream. When he calmed down, he related how, in all his life, he had only seen his father but once and just for a fleeting moment, at that. He had grown up with his mother and other siblings, all of whom had fathers different from his. Every time he inquired about his father, his mother would go silent or change the topic.

Then, the pastor related that one day, while sitting on the front steps of his home, eating a meal, a man rode into the yard and held a brief conversation with his mother before riding off again. Engrossed in eating his meal, he did not pay much attention to the man. However, after the man rode off, to his horror, his mother said to him, "That was your father to whom I was just speaking." He dropped his plate of food and ran out onto the street, but only managed to see the back of the stranger, as he rode off into the distance. Needless to say, he never saw the stranger again. But, then, since he did not see the stranger's face that day, he could have passed him every day from that time and he would have been none the wiser.

The tears really began to flow, when he described the devastation that the experience caused to his personality. He became reticent and rebellious and began experiencing serious retardation in his academic performance. However, the worst fallout from the incident was that he became delusional, creating this imaginary person whom he regarded as his father. When he got into his bed, at night, he would often hold long conversations with this phantom, telling him about his pains and his plans. That would make him feel safe and strong, in his own private world.

As long as he had kept it in the privacy of his thoughts, it would have been alright. However, his delusion began to spill over into his public persona. Whenever there were discussions about fathers at school he would be in the thick of things, relating fantastic stories about playing games, and going fishing and taking hunting trips with his 'father'. He would write essays and short stories in which he would recount the adventures that he had with his father' on weekends and during vacation times.

By this time, this powerful man of God was trembling as he lamented that every time he told the stories about his father', whether by speaking or writing, a deep sense of guilt and condemnation would come over him. Yet, he seemed powerless to stop. He was now in his thirties, anointed and, seemingly, well set to take off in ministry. However, what had begun as an escape hatch for his pain, in childhood, had now become a compulsion to exaggerate or lie, which was threatening to abort his destiny. He shouted, "Prophet, I need deliverance! Help me, please!"

- Thereupon, I asked him to forgive: his mother for not leveling with him on the identity of his father;
- his father for abandoning and rejecting him
- himself for heaping blame and condemnation upon himself for what his mother and father had done to him
- God for thinking that He did not care about him.

By the time he was finished, he had screamed and coughed up legions of demons that had taken pos session of his soul all those years. He now looked at me as though he was in a different world. He talked of feeling brand new and free for the first time, since the day of the incident. He left the session that day, ready to pursue his destiny with renewed vigor. The last time I saw him, he was releasing some powerful revelations on his television program on one of our local stations.

I cited this case study because, in essence, our brother is not alone in this problem. Exaggeration (lying), on the part of leaders, is an all-too-frequent occurrence, when a move of God kicks in. It is like an epidemic and it must be addressed before the next outbreak of Holy Ghost fire at your location. In fact, right now, by God's authority, I release an anointing to break every tendency within you to fall prey to this practice. Receive your deliverance, now!

Many leaders, in their exuberance and excitement at what is happening, inadvertently overestimate (I give them the benefit of the doubt) the sizes of the crowds attending services, the number of decisions for salvation, the number of miracles and the financial intake or expenses. However, there are also those who knowingly manipulate the statistics in a deliberate effort to loom large in the eyes of the public and lure more people to the meetings. With seemingly no qualms about being untruthful, they nonchalantly turn a crowd of one thousand into fifteen hundred or even 'close to two thousand'. Fifty people, standing at the altar, easily become 'seventy five to one hundred decisions'. Five testimonies about healing get reported as 'dozens of miracles are taking place.' A need for $2000 is pitched, during offering time as, 'We have a deficit of thousands of dollars that must be met tonight or we may have to close the meetings.'

However, such a practice runs contrary to the essence of Kingdom living, which is built on truthfulness. It is also counterproductive to the spirit within which God releases His fire among His people—every new move of God is really a fresh revelation of truth. To engage in the numbers game, in the midst of such a release, is to tempt both fate and God, at the basest level. Yet, that is not the worst aspect of this whole sordid affair.

You see, whereas God may take not-too-drastic steps to bring correction, Satan and the critics are not that kind. What those who engage in this practice ought to know is that exaggeration, over estimation or lies (that is what they really are) open the way for the Serpent Spirit to enter the fertile gardens of our minds or Eden, as it were, one more time. He is a major player in the Kingdom of darkness and a master of disguises. His burning passion is to discredit God by quenching every fire that God ignites in the earth, just as he did back in Eden. Therefore, he brings with him the spirits of compromise, deception and rebellion against God's purpose. As long as he is accommodated, he will set off flares over the ministry that will beckon the critics to come calling.

That is exactly what happened with moves of God of recent vintage. Critics, attracted by the fantastic claims made in press releases, concerning what was taking place in the meetings, came calling not necessarily to compile data on what was happening, but primarily to check out the claims, whether they were true or not. In many instances, to the shame of the ministries, in question, and I dare say to that of the Church in general, many of the claims were found to be erroneous. Needless to say, the critics had a field day when they published their findings in the media.

In each case, this negative publicity had a profound effect on the momentum of progress for the specific move of God. The credibility of leader ship came into serious question. Many people felt deceived. In their minds, it was as though there was a deliberate attempt by someone to insult their intelligence. The result was that the crowds stopped coming and together with that, the offerings became smaller, truly leaving deficits of gigantic proportions. This also contributed to the demise of those moves of God.

I implore you, when that wave of God's glory hits your neck of the woods, be honest and truthful in your response to the hand of God at work. Do not let excitement and exuberance get the better of you. You do not have to manipulate statistics to try to create an impression or to attract people. The sheer presence of God and your obedience to His instructions will draw people to the house of God. You must remember that in every sphere of life, both spiritually and in the natural, credibility and integrity are your most valuable assets. Guard them with your life.

Lying is an abomination to God. It is no surprise, then, that where exaggeration, deliberate overestimation and the stretching of the truth are allowed to flourish, the channels through which God pours out His Spirit to fuel the fire become blocked. Starved for fuel, the flames begin to die, ever so slowly. If correct measures are not applied within reasonable time, then, that which the people of God fasted and prayed for, over many years, dies an untimely death.

"How wonderful it is, how pleasant, when brothers live together in harmony! For harmony is as precious as the fragrant anointing oil..."
(Psalms 133:1&2, NLT).

Life Saving Fuel For The Anointing Fire

We dedicated the previous chapter to the vital task of identifying and profiling the elements that can destroy any move of God. Let us now look at some of the steps that leaders of every move of God can take to ensure its longevity. Remember the watchword for the season is: Whatever I obtain, I must maintain, in order to retain.

Teamwork

The counter measure to Egotism is Teamwork. When properly administered, instead of some star boy vying for the ascendancy, one sees the emergence of a captain who gives leadership, not so much by way of political appointment, but more so through influence, generated by the anointing that is upon him. It is important to note that influence is as great as or sometimes, even a greater force than position in determining the direction that a move of God takes. Every leader, therefore, must seek to increase his influence with members of the congregation. If he recognizes that there are members who seem to be wielding more influence than him in the group. It will be to his advantage to incorporate them into the leadership structure that gives direction to the movement. Failure to do so may bring retardation or possibly, stagnation to the move of God.

The book of Acts provides strong evidence of the virtues of Teamwork in the way that the Apostles conducted the affairs of the early Church. Here is a shortlist of them:

- Teamwork attracts the anointing that ignites and sustains the fire of God -...they were all with one accord in one place... Then there appeared to them divided tongues, as of fire, and one sat upon each of them. (Acts 2:1-3, NKJV). Teamwork is a vital tool for evangelism—those who accepted his message were baptized, and about three thousand were added to their number that day. (Acts 2:41, NIV)
- Teamwork creates an atmosphere of fellow ship—they devoted themselves to the apostles' teaching and to the fellowship, to the breaking of bread and to prayer. (Acts 2:42, NIV).
- Teamwork generates the power for the working of miracles, signs and wonders—everyone was filled with awe, and many wonders and miraculous signs were done by the apostles. (Acts 2:43).
- Teamwork levels the playing field in the house of God: Race, class and gender discrimination find no place for expression- All the believers were together and had everything in common. Selling their possessions and goods, they gave to anyone as he had need. Every day they continued to meet together in the temple courts. They broke bread in their homes and ate together with gladness and sincere hearts, (Acts 2:44-46, NIV).
- Teamwork is a master key to sustainable Church growth - And the Lord added to their number daily those who were being saved. (Acts 2:47, NIV).
- Teamwork creates a platform for proper division of labor-So the Twelve gathered all the disciples together and said, "It would not be right for us to neglect the ministry of the word

of God in order to wait on tables. 3 Brothers, choose seven men from among you who are known to be full of the Spirit and wisdom. We will turn this responsibility over to them 4 and will give our attention to prayer and the ministry of the word." (Acts 6:2-4, NIV).

Over the years, too many moves of God have had to endure ridicule because many of the leaders and worshippers indulged in weird actions, claiming to be led by the Holy Spirit. Some have crawled on the floor like snakes, others have barked like dogs and yet others have been heard to cackle like chickens, justifying their behavior with the expression, 'I was just obeying the Spirit.' Is it that God will not give such instructions? It is quite possible. However, when the practice becomes the norm instead of the exception and when it takes the focus away from God and unto the individual, it becomes a most appropriate time for other members of the team to step in and bring wisdom to bear on the situation.

In other instances, people have walked off their jobs, stating that the Lord told them not to work, yet not having a clue as to how they would finance their lives from that point. Eventually they became a bur den to others. There are also those who have refused to send their children to school because with the new anointing flowing, they sensed that this was the last move before Jesus returned, hence education would be of no value. What all of the above needed was wise counsel that teamwork provides. You see, there is a very thin line between faith and foolishness.

Where teamwork is allowed to operate freely, extremism and weird behavior will find it difficult to rear their ugly heads. Teamwork provides a system of checks and balances, to keep the movement from being overrun or strangled by weirdoes and extremists. Such persons are known to surf the Church circuit, seizing upon fresh moves of God as ideal staging areas for their folly.

Every major instruction that carries the potential to affect the ministry is set before the team, so that there is consensus as to timing and method of approach before implementation. Some extremists may dismiss this as grieving the Spirit, trying to control God or even disobedience to God. However, as I indicated earlier, one must understand that God sends the water, which floods the river, but it is our responsibility to raise the banks, so that the flood does not get out of hand and wreak havoc on the landscape. The wise man, Solomon, celebrates the value of teamwork, in this way, "...in an abundance of counselors there is victory and safety." (Proverbs 24:6, AMP).

Notwithstanding the virtues of teamwork, keeping it operational is not an easy task. The truth is that it is its very virtues that draw negative fire from the enemy. I remember when a team of us started ministry in the early 90's, many seasoned ministers, driven by ignorance and blatant jealousy attacked the idea with expressions such as, 'You cannot have more than one leader running a ministry. Anything with more than one head is a monster.' What they did not see was that this was the pattern of the early Church, where leadership was plural in nature. Peter, James, John and the other apostles did not jostle one another for political position. Instead, they led by the power generated by collective responsibility and influence.

In spite of such scathing remarks, we worked together as a team. God allowed us to acquire properties, establish branches, make national and international impact and flow in a phenomenal anointing for signs, wonders and miracles. All of this happened within the first ten years of our existence. Many of those detractors, some of whom were in minis try since we were teenagers, are still struggling to acquire their first piece of property.

Another strategy that the enemy uses is to attack the team from within. He aims his guns at the intricate mechanics that empower the team-elements such as mutual respect, sharing, caring, communication and friendship. He targets one member of the team into whom he deposits, by way of suggestion, the thought that the measure of success being enjoyed has come about because he is doing the lion's share of the work. Were it not for his expertise. Popularity, education and anointing, nothing would have been done.

Suddenly egotism, the very spirit against which teamwork is the greatest defense, enters the picture. It dupes that team member to begin doing things on his own, implementing programs and formulating policy without consultation, spending monies without approval and inserting the deadly 'I' instead of We' in his expressions. It is now his agenda and vision that become the point of focus, as distinct from that of the team.

From the moment this poison dart takes effect, the whole move of God begins to feel the strain. The atmosphere of 'one accord' becomes corrupted with contentions, personality conflicts, spurious allegations and suspicions. Any attempt to point out that irregularity to the individual is misconstrued as a personal attack. He usually counters by labeling the rest of the team as the real trouble makers. When left unchecked this spirit becomes a sure flame killer and the movement that began with such great momentum grinds to an excruciatingly painful halt.

My prophetic proclamation over every move of God is that the leaders will see virtue in putting legs to Psalms 133. It is that unity, as manifested in team work, which generates the anointing, which fuels the fire that propels the move of God from glory to glory to glory.

The Absolute Necessity of Prophetic Teaching

One of the most misunderstood and misused gifts of the Spirit is Prophecy. Consequently, many Church leaders have either taken a wide berth around it or have rejected it outright. They claim that it carries no relevance in today's Church. Others who have embraced it are handling it with kids' gloves, at best. They fall prey to the syndrome that makes people fear what they do not understand; condemn what they do not like and seek to destroy what they cannot control. Yet, it is an irrefutable truth that no move of God has ever come into operation without prophecy playing a major role. May I also add that no move of God can maintain its momentum, purity, dynamism and advancement without a continuous flow of prophetic revelation?

Now, having functioned in the office of the Prophet for over two decades and having also been an eye witness to prophetic happenings (or is it mishaps, in so many cases!) for many more years than that, I will be the first to admit that many people have done some dumb things over the years, under the guise of prophecy. Due to lack of understanding of this most precious gift of the Spirit, many of God's people have:

- Been robbed of huge fortunes of money and property by unscrupulous prophets. Married the wrong partner because someone claimed to have seen a prophetic vision in which God revealed the match.
- Quit their jobs or lost their businesses because they followed the unwise counsel of a prophet.
- Gone into apostasy and even bordered on idolatry because they trusted the prophetic integrity of their leaders.
- Started ministry and failed because they thought they had a word from God.
- Been walking in condemnation because of the warped picture of God and of themselves that some intercessor, parading as one who hears from God, has etched on their psyche.
- Become so spiritual that they see a demon behind every tree and sin in every church.

The list is inexhaustible and what is so lamentable is that, day after day, it continues to expand. If one were to look at the situation on a case by case basis, the stories will make one's stomach go into convulsions. The fallout is even worse, in that, a great number of victims and their close relations have turned away from God permanently. It will take a miracle of gigantic proportions to restore their faith in God and in the Church.

Notwithstanding the above, I proclaim, without fear of contradiction, that Prophecy is integral to the initiation, sustenance and advancement of every move of God in every season. Its misuse and abuse by unscrupulous ministers cannot justify throwing out the baby with the bath water. It is like deciding not to travel by air because there was a plane crash—one plane crash does not bring down all other airplanes.

When administered according to God's directives. Prophecy is a most powerful channel of enrichment for the Church. You see, Prophecy, in its purest form, places the Prophet and the hearer on God's broadcast frequency. At that level, one becomes privy to the unfolding of the mind of God. It is only when the Church knows the mind of God for the season and is willing to obey what He says, that we will be able to remain relevant to the times and maximize the impact of His Kingdom upon the world's system.

Yes, contrary to the mindset of religious folks, the underlying purpose for a move of God, in the earth, is not necessarily to bring thrills, goose pimples, miracles, signs, wonders and increase in the size of congregations. Those are the fringe benefits that naturally follow the fire. They also function as tools to accomplish a more important divine purpose. When God releases that special grace upon a people, He has radical transformation on His mind- trans formation of individuals, families, communities and even nations. More than this, He also has a step by step plan on how to accomplish this.

It stands to reason, then, that:

- Whereas, prophecy is the means through which God downloads His mind to us, and
- whereas, God's intention, with every new release of the anointing, is to radically transform individuals and societies and
- whereas, it is in the unfolding of God's mind that we discover His step by step plan for accomplishing this and
- whereas, it is only when we follow His plan that we can be effective,

Let it be known that no move of God or people of God will be able to make a sustainable impact in the earth without the power that authentic prophetic ministry brings.

Here is an abridged list that highlights the great value that God has attached to prophecy:

- For the entire creation week, it was prophecy that God used to restore order and life to the earth that 'was without form and void.'(Genesis I).
- Prophetic proclamation was the instrument of freedom that brought deliverance to Israel from slavery in Pharaoh's Egypt. (Exodus 3–12).
- It is the prophetic word that brings sustenance to the spirit of man. (Deuteronomy 8:3).
- God uses prophecy to reveal the secrets of His Kingdom to His people. (Deuteronomy 29:29 & Matthew 13).
- God makes no move in the earth until He reveals it to His servants, the prophets. (Amos 3:7).
- Jesus used prophetic revelation to establish the strong foundational principles upon which he continues to build his Church. (Matthew 16:18&19).

Since prophecy is the channel through which God releases fresh revelation to His Church, then, prophetic teaching has to be a most powerful tool by which He upgrades and updates its knowledge base, concerning Kingdom principles, thus keeping it relevant to the changing times and seasons.

Daniel, himself a master prophet, did say that "the people that do know their God will be strong and do exploits." (Daniel 11:32, KJV). The word 'know' gives rise to the word 'knowledge'. A closer look at both words will determine that they are built on 'now, as their foundation. Therein lies an ultra-explosive truth: Knowledge is only effective, if it is based on information that is in the 'now' or up to date.

It is clear, then, that Daniel recognized that the strength of any people rests on what actions they take to consistently update and upgrade their knowledge-base concerning God. As a prophet, Daniel, no doubt, would recommend to us that the best action to take is to position ourselves where fresh prophetic revelation of God is flowing from God. It is guaranteed to keep us relevant to the times, en courant with the changing world in which we live and in sync with the mind of God, concerning His next step.

Jesus understood this principle very clearly. It is no wonder, then, that he employed it with great effect, during his ministry in the earth. He had come at a time when Israel had become stuck in a religious quagmire that drew its substance (or is it lack of substance :) from Moses' Law. In essence, that document had not been updated since the days when Israel was going through the wilderness. Consequently, the religion of the day was not relevant to the reality of life in the society of the day.

Jesus set about to change this. Hence the reason why Jesus would often preface his teachings with the expression, "You have heard that it was said to those of old… But I say to you…"Nowhere, in Jesus teachings, did he use this expression in a more emphatic way than in Matthew 5-7, the passage of scripture, which must be regarded as the constitution document for the conduct of life in the Kingdom of God. Jesus' aim, here, was to update the laws that had made life in Israel an experience in dead, oppressive legalism. In their place, he intended to establish Kingdom principles that would upgrade the quality of life (for those who chose to live by them) by infusing new spirit into the dry blandness that marked man's relationship with God and with his fellowman. Here are two clear cut examples:

> *You have heard that it was said to those of old, You shall not murder, and whoever murders will be in danger of the judgment. 22 But I say to you that whoever is angry with his brother without a cause shall be in danger of the judgment. (Matthew 5:21–22, NKJV). Again you have heard that it was said to those of old, You shall not swear falsely, but shall perform your oaths to the Lord.' 34 But I say to you, do not swear at all: neither by heaven, for it is God's throne. (Matthew 5:33–34, NKJV).*

What was the source from which Jesus drew such revelation? What made him believe that he had the authority to overlay these revelations upon the previously untouchable Laws of Moses? Without a doubt, Jesus had to have drawn his power and authority from his Father in heaven, via the prophetic hookup that he enjoyed.

On one occasion, the leaders of the Jews challenged Jesus as to his right to call himself the Son of God, to break the traditions of Moses and thus, to precipitate a new move of God. Jesus, unphased by their efforts to intimidate him, identified the source of his authority, in this way: "The Son can do nothing of himself, but what he seeth the Father do:...30 I can of mine own self do nothing: as I hear, I judge:... because I seek not mine own will, but the will of the Father which hath sent me." (John 5:19& 30, KJV). He was stating, in no uncertain terms, that his teachings were prophetic in nature - a direct download from the Father.

To say that the prophetic teachings, which Jesus delivered, impacted his world is to make the understatement of the ages. The evidence is as overwhelming as it is irrefutable. They were both the catalyst and the fuel for a new movement that is still transforming mindsets from legalism to Kingdom living and from religion to revelation. The truth is that every new move of God, since those days and for the foreseeable future, is really a fresh look at the very Kingdom principles that Jesus laid down by way of prophetic revelation, in his day.

Therefore, it will be an exercise in futility for any leader of a move of God, today and in the future, to deny the place of prophetic teaching as a fuel source for maintaining its momentum and propelling it forward. The fire will become starved for fuel and die a painful death.

Every leader of God's people should know, then, that when the fire of God breaks out in his locale, if he is not disposed to flow prophetically, he is obliged to bring in proven prophets, on a regular basis to stoke the fire with the release of fresh revelation. If he is teachable, he too will soon experience a prophetic flow within his spirit. It will not only pave the way for God to rise up prophets from among the people, but it will also infuse new life in both the church and the wider community. Of course, it will be of absolute necessity and the responsibility of leadership to provide proper teaching and mentoring for those so anointed. This is to minimize the possibility of false prophecy and weird behavior becoming a distraction from the main focus—the glory of God.

Finally, Apostle Paul, who testified to the fact that when God called him, he spent over three years in the Arabian desert, receiving prophetic download from God (Galatians 1:15-19), warned that we should not despise prophesying. To do so would be to disconnect ourselves from the mind of God, precipitating stagnation and death of a people and of the fire that God has ignited among them. (1 Thessalonians 5:20). The truth is that in the prescription he gave to the Corinthians for rescuing the move of God that had been reeling under the attack of the enemy and to get it going again, Apostle Paul admonished them to choose and learn to flow in Prophecy, the best gift of the Spirit-(1 Corinthians 14:1, NKJV): "Pursue love, and desire spiritual gifts, but especially that you may prophesy."

Uncompromising Obedience

Quite recently, I had the honor of being one of the speakers at a breakfast meeting for Pastors. One of the other speakers released a word that confirmed what the Lord has been saying to us in the Caribbean, for some years now. He told how God had instructed him to leave London, where he lives, to come to the Caribbean for a season, because there is going to be an outbreak of God's fire, in the region, in phenomenal proportions. He had already visited over seven Caribbean nations, helping to sensitize pastors and intercessors of our responsibility to birth the new move. Needless to say, the prophetic proclamation was received with great excitement, especially in light of the fact that it coincided with a similar prophecy that had been uttered by a world renowned minister, only a matter of days prior to the conference.

Amidst all the excitement, the host pastor asked all present to kneel and observe a few minutes of silence. The idea was to show gratitude to God for Him thinking that we, in the Caribbean, are worthy of such a move of His Spirit and to demonstrate our commitment to humble ourselves in anticipation of its manifestation. A full minute had hardly passed, when the silence was shattered by the heartfelt cries of ministers reaching out to God. Some were repenting. Others were speaking in tongues. Yet, others were laid out flat on the floor, weeping bitterly for personal shortcomings.

As the cries rose to a crescendo, the Lord quickened, within my spirit, a prophetic word that seemed totally out of character with the proceedings. Nevertheless, I sought the permission of the host who opened the door for me to deliver it. Here it is, in part:

> My children do not make the same mistake that others have made, in times past, and killed the fire, which I had lit among them. Do not become emotionally attached to the move of My Spirit. Emotions only serve to create a thrill, but may cloud your vision from focusing on the main thing: making a conscious effort to continuously obey My instructions. What moves me is not your cries of repentance, while you are on the floor; but your acts of obedience, when you leave here, today. If you have been praying and not obeying, it is time to stop praying and start obeying my instructions. It is by your obedience to My instructions that you will see the answers to your prayers unfold. Others asked Me for fire, in times past. I gave it to them. Then, they stopped obeying My instructions and the fire went out. When I light this fire among you, in the Caribbean, it must be for a lasting memorial to the rest of the world and for the generations to come. I work with those who obey me. Perpetual obedience is greater than the sacrifice of fasting, prayer, spiritual warfare and other related activities. In the past, many have spent years petitioning me for revival fire, only to quench it within a short time, due to disobedience. Obey Me and the fire will never go out.'

Immediately, the crying ceased. All present had suddenly wizened up to the truth that, far from being an emotional ride, when the fire of God breaks out among a people, there is a grave responsibility upon them to walk in obedience to Him. Praying and fasting may ignite the fire, but it is continuous obedience that will sustain it.

At the end of the day's proceedings, a minister, visiting from Wales, came to me teary-eyed. He expressed his gratitude to me for having been bold enough to declare the word of the Lord, even in the light of what was happening at the time. Yet, he lamented the fact that such a word was not spoken in Wales, where the Church has been praying for the last 100 years for God to rekindle a fire that had broken out across the land, in 1904, but had come to naught, within a mere eighteen months. He left the meeting prepared to go back to Wales and proclaim the message of obedience to the intercessors. I wait with baited breath to hear about what will transpire in Wales, in the near future.

- When we pray, God sends the answer wrapped up in a set of instructions.
- Every act of obedience causes the answer to unfold one layer at a time. The instructions that I am willing to obey will determine the quality of the life that I desire to live.

Money

Although we will look at the God's position on the economic empowerment of His people in greater detail, in a later chapter, allow me, at this juncture, to address the question of money, as it pertains to maintaining the momentum of a move of God.

Moses gave Israel a most amazing instruction, in Deuteronomy 8:18, AMP:

> But you shall (earnestly) remember the Lord your God, for it is He Who gives you power to get wealth that He may establish His covenant which He swore to your fathers, as it is this day.

This admonition came within the context of Moses preparing Israel for the impending move of God that would catapult them out of wilderness living into Promised Land living in Canaan. Even before Israel left Egypt, God had promised that He would bring them to a place that was flowing with milk and honey. That was, in essence, an analogy for economic prosperity, which would be a mark of God's benevolence towards them.

Now that Israel was poised, both in time and place to enter Canaan, after forty years of wandering, Moses was reminding them that, in the new sea son up ahead, God would release an anointing upon them, not only to conquer their enemies, but also, to empower them for acquiring houses, land, livestock and everything needful to lead a life of economic abundance. However, they were never to think that the change in their fortunes would come by way of their own intelligence and skills. Rather, they were to remember that it was God who gave them the power (anointing) to get wealth.

A set of fundamental truths flows out of this. They are very instructive for every leader and his congregation that gets caught up in a tsunami of God's glory:

- God wants His people to be wealthy.
- God has an anointing available that empowers His people to get wealth.
- When God releases the anointing that initiates and sustains the momentum of a new move, the power to generate wealth is an integral part of it.
- Wealth generation is a provision of the divine covenant.
- Built into wealth generation is the power for wealth management.
- Wealth is a sign of God's covenant with us.
- Wealth is necessary for establishing the divine covenant.
- Being wealthy is neither sinful nor carnal, per see.

It stands to reason, then, that every leader of a move of God must adjust his thinking towards wealth generation and towards his relationship with money if it is God who releases the anointing for wealth generation, wealth accumulation and wealth management, then why is there such foreboding on the part of Church leaders when the question of money arises? Moses said that God uses wealth as one of the pillars on which to establish His covenant with us. It means, then, that in any major release of anointing in a congregation, there will also be an increase in the potential of that congregation to accumulate wealth. It follows naturally, then, that both the leaders and the people should prepare themselves to properly handle such a scenario.

In light of such irrefutable evidence of God's endorsement of and empowerment to generate wealth, why would a ministry find itself deep in debt, during and after the season that saw an evident fire of God, burning in the midst of the congregation? One ministry in which the fire of God burned for more than six years, in recent times, is now struggling to service a debt of over $9.5mil US. The answer has to lie in the attitude that leadership adopts towards money:

> There seems to be two distinct positions that Church leaders hold on the issue of wealth/money, in ordinary times, which become even more accentuated, when the anointing fire breaks out among a people. They are on opposite ends of the pole: (1) fear of wealth/money or (2) uncontrolled lust for wealth/money.

Those leaders who fear wealth are primarily ignorant of the true purpose of wealth generation, as highlighted above: Wealth is one of the pillars upon which God establishes His covenant with His people. They are also driven by a desire for self-preservation under the scrutiny of negative public opinion. Their rationale seems to be that if they project a picture of being perpetually in lack, no one will be able to accuse them of stealing church funds or exploiting the people. Little do they know, though, that, guilty or not, such stigmatization comes with the territory. Their responsibility is to ensure that they are not guilty as accused

Additionally, such leaders seem to have factored into their philosophy of ministry an erroneous interpretation of 1 Timothy 6:10, which state that the love of money is the root of all evil. Their reckoning of this verse appears to state that money is the root of all evil, effectively demonizing money as something to be shunned. Therefore, in their quest to be counted righteous, they have stymied the anointing for wealth generation and have embraced poverty and lack as indicators of holiness and piety. However, there are six important truths of which they must become cognizant:

- Although poverty and lack are not sins, per se, they sure can create occasions for sin. This is so because wherever they hold sway, people have the tendency to rob God in their tithes and offerings. Malachi calls that a sin, which can surely incur the wrath of God (Malachi 3).
- The spirit of the leader is the dominant spirit in any arena where humanity gathers. If the leader operates under a spirit of poverty and lack, then. The people will experience grave difficulties generating enough wealth to meet their personal needs and those of the ministry.
- Where people have difficulty in meeting their needs, there is neither cheerfulness nor spontaneity in their giving. Consequently, these very leaders tend to turn offering time into an occasion for begging, cajoling, and sometimes intimidation of the congregation, in their effort to extract money from the people to pay for expenses.
- Regardless of the measure of the anointing that a leader carries, a loud Hallelujah or a burst of unknown tongues, at the checkout counter of a supermarket or hardware, does not pay the bills. It still takes money to advance a vision, acquire property, and meet current expenses, finance expansion, sponsor missionary and evangelism programs and so on.
- When the question arises concerning how a bill is to be paid, money provides the answer (Ecclesiastes 10:19).
- Money is a great defense against lack in the ministry and against embarrassment in the market place (Ecclesiastes 7:12).

On the other end of the pole, are the leaders who are driven by greed or an uncontrolled lust for money. Their philosophy dictates that they can never have enough of it. Consequently, they devise a myriad of schemes by which they could constantly extract money from the people of God. They think nothing of turning offering time into an occasion for financial abuse and exploitation. Often, they try to justify their action with a well placed "Thus saith the Lord.'

How many times have we been to conferences or regular church services at which the pastor, the speaker or a minister, noted for having a special anointing for taking offerings, use one of the following lines of approach?

- A play on the digits of the current year: The Lord is telling me that we should give $2006 - $1 for each year. In 2001, I was in a conference at which a visiting pastor, purporting to have heard from God, announced that the offering should be $201 for that night. My heart went out for him, as he went from row to row, targeting individuals with the question, "$201, is it you, is it you?" Out of a congregation of over five hundred persons that night, not one person responded. Needless to say, to save face, he dropped the ceiling to $20 (to drop from the 201st floor to the 20th, with such speed, can cause serious back and neck pains). It was only then that people began putting money in the receptacle. My question is this, "Did God really says?" My thinking is that if God had really spoken, there would have been at least one per son, even that pastor himself, who would have responded to the original request.
- Inflation of the real amount, when there is designated giving: The rationale is that, given the possibility of a substantial percentage of the people not having much to give, the rest will feel challenged by the big figure to give more. In the end, although the giving may not reach the inflated target, it will at least come close to the real amount. In a previous segment, we identified such an approach as lying. God will be hard pressed to bless it.
- Attempting to impact other people by the accuracy with which one hears from God: In pursuit of this, they challenge the congregation to give amounts that can only be described

as ridiculous. On one occasion, I heard a preacher who was given the liberty to raise her own honorarium tell the congregation that the Lord was leading her to ask for an offering of $37.01. In the first place, unless the person is paying by credit or debit card, it is hardly likely that anyone will have that exact sum. Furthermore, and I dare say even more crucial, is the possibility of people acting in disobedience to God, if they give an amount that is different.

- Imposing a sense of guilt or fear on people, so that they give as a means of salving their con sciences: This ploy seems to work with great effectiveness because few people want to incur the wrath of God for giving too little or for not giving at all.
- Spurious promises that create false hopes of instant returns on offerings given: They deliberately twist John 6:38 to read, 'Give and good measure shall be given back to you instantly.' However, people are deprived of vital information, pertaining to Kingdom economics, such as: (1). Giving attracts the favor of God to our lives. How we process the favor is what determines the level of manifestation of blessings that accrue to us. (2). Honest, diligent work is still God's preferred channel for prospering His people. (3). According to 2 Corinthians 9:1-12, the giving of offerings is akin to planting seeds. Seeds need time to germinate and grow before they mature into trees that bear fruit. (4). God's people are his trees of righteousness. Each tree brings forth fruit in its own season. Therefore to promise instant returns to everyone is to indulge in false hood, as well as to generate grave frustrations in people's lives. (s). The truth is that for every one hundred people in an auditorium, only one may get the letter with the check for the large amount of money, on reaching home. The rest will have to work for it, over a period of time.
- Making prophetic declarations over people according to how much they give: Over the years, many mighty men and women of God have lost direction and have even come to ruin, because of this practice. It corrupts the purity and contradicts the ultimate purpose of the gifts of the Spirit,

as outlined by Apostle Paul in I Corinthians 12:7,NLT - A spiritual gift is given to each of us as a means of helping the entire Church. This practice is a sure recipe for disaster, if introduced into any arena where the fire of God is burning. It is nothing less than witchcraft.

In light of the above, what, then, should be the approach used by leaders of a move of God to handle wealth in such a season? They must seek to understand and embrace the following truths:

Wealth generation, prosperity and money are all God's idea

The first time that God spoke to man, in Genesis 1:28, NKJV, He commanded man to "Be fruitful and multiply..." The Message Bible renders this same instruction this way, "Prosper! Reproduce..." Based on the Law of First Mention, it means that God expects us to prosper.

Be a giver: give and be seen to give

The leader of a move of God must always strive to be the biggest giver in the congregation. In the process of him doing so, his spirit flows down to the people and greatly encourages them to give, in their turn. Such a practice is even more effective, when the leader makes his giving visible—at offering time, he too walks to the receptacle area and deposits his offerings in the container in plain sight of all present.

Plant seeds in other ministries

Leadership should be on the lookout for worthy causes being pursued by other ministries, such as a building project or a community outreach program, into which to make monetary contributions. The law of sowing and reaping works to great effect, here, as well. However, there is a word of caution.

Many ministries have developed a dangerous practice of seeing a prospering ministry as their Jireh, instead of trusting God for His favor and strategies for creating a greater cash flow of their own. Consequently, as soon as those leaders discern that a particular ministry has begun to experience financial prosperity, they begin to send begging letters for funds to help in anything from purchasing property to staging a pastor's appreciation day. What such leaders need to realize is that the same God who is blessing the prosperous church is also willing to do the same for them. The key to it all, though, will be in their willingness to obey God's instructions, specific to their situation.

Additionally, such leaders must also understand that giving flows naturally out of relationship. As such, they should seek to establish strong relationships with other leaders before dispatching their passionate begging letters. In the same token, they must appreciate the fact that the other pastor reserves the right to give or not to give. Therefore, if he chooses not to give that does not make him a heathen.

> Every leader must know that money was made for him and not him for money.

A leader should be in control of money and not let money control him. It means that he does not have to indulge in or involve the congregation in network marketing schemes and other risky investments to generate a proper cash flow, individually or corporately. If members wish to get involved in such schemes, it should be an entirely private and personal decision that they make. A pastor will be putting his good name and integrity on the line, as well as creating an atmosphere for blame and mistrust. If he takes on the role of organizer and the scheme were to fall apart shortly thereafter.

I remember a situation in which the pastor of a ministry, which was experiencing a strong move of God, invested a tidy sum of ministry funds into a network marketing scheme, only to see the pyramid crash soon afterwards. Needless to say the loss was devastating. The result was that the ministry could no longer service payments on a sizeable building that it was renting with a view to purchase and had to move to smaller facilities. This set the pursuit of the vision back many years. Additionally, accusations and rumors, as to the whereabouts of the money, spread like wild fire and triggered an exodus from the ministry of many long standing members.

If we were to take the principle of controlling money vs. being controlled by money a little further, it will lead us to address the question of pastors borrowing money from members of the congregation for personal use. That is a definite 'No! No!' and a sure recipe for disaster, in any season and especially during the time of the outpouring. Such a course of action will compromise his authority as it pertains to disciplinary matters on the part of the lender, his relatives, friends and everyone else who becomes privy to the information. It will also belie the truth of the message that the pastor is preaching. He cannot be talking about God's ability to supply the needs of His people and at the same time be looking to a member of the congregation to supply his. It will raise serious questions about his integrity, especially if he cannot meet the repayment schedule on time or downright refuses to repay, as has happened in so many instances.

Recently, I heard of a case in point. A pastor borrowed a tidy sum of money from a member of the congregation with the agreement that he will repay it in monthly installments of a particular amount. Unfortunately, he broke the agreement. On a lump sum of thousands of dollars, he has so far been offering only $100 dollars, whenever he could get it. On each occasion that the member has approached him for payment, he has either offered the excuse of being strapped for cash or being too busy to speak with her. Well, she has now left the ministry and has made it her business to tell as many people as possible about the situation. To compound the issue, the pastor seems unmoved, while others are also making their exodus from the ministry because of the matter.

My take on this matter is that such a situation should be avoided altogether by not engaging in this practice in the first place. Pastor will be better off going to the bank or some other financial institution for a loan. This will guarantee him repaying money in a timely manner. However, if it be unavoidable that he has to borrow from a member then both parties must observe proper business principles by drawing up a written agreement, witnessed by a third party who has some legal training. Above all, the man of God must honor the agreement. He will do well to observe this principle of life:

> Honor and integrity are a man's greatest assets. Guard yours with your life.

Dethrone money from its exalted position

Although money has been accredited with having the answer for all things, it is also true that God has provided a way to acquire things without money. The truth is that it will accrue to our greater good to not only acquainting ourselves with it, but also, to make it a practice of ours.

Isaiah 55:1, AMP, admonishes, "...everyone who is thirsty! Come to the waters; and he who has no money, come, buy and eat! Yes, come, buy (priceless, spiritual) wine and milk without money and without price (simply for the self-surrender that accepts the blessing)." The Psalmist, David, although having unlimited access to money, also found a way to dethrone money from its pedestal, in his quest to acquire things. He reveals his secret in Psalms 37:4, AMP, "Delight yourself also in the Lord, and He will give you the desires and secret petitions of your heart." When Jesus walked the earth, he also dealt with the issue. In Matthew 6:33, AMP, he exhorts, "But seek (aim at and strive after) first of all His Kingdom and His righteousness (His way of doing and being right), and then all these things taken together will be given you besides." Isaiah's call for self-surrender, David's advice to delight in God and Jesus' counsel to seek God as priority, are all expressions synonymous with one word - OBEDIENCE.

So, the secret is out: In the Kingdom of God, obedience is a higher medium of exchange than money. It means, then, that no leader should allow money, or the lack of it, to retard or prevent him from pursuing the vision that God has mandated for him to establish. By making it a practice to obey God without compromise, all relevant resources will be at his disposal. Here is a Kingdom advisory: Position yourself where God wants you to be and He will give you access to all that you need to have.

Exercise financial prudence

Proverbs 28:20, AMP, admonishes that "A faithful man shall abound with blessings, but he who makes haste to be rich (at any cost) shall not go unpunished." This should be ample warning for every leader of a move of God to act prudently in handling the rap idly increasing funds that come with the outpouring of the Spirit.

A leader must understand the difference between being ultimately responsible for the finances of the church, in the role of manager or steward, and being the owner, with unlimited freedom to dispose of them as he wishes. As manager, he is expected to implement appropriate accounting and management procedures for proper disbursement of monies that come in. He will be well advised to employ a qualified administrator, preferably one who is from within the congregation and who has proven to be trustworthy. He must know that ministry consists of the spiritual dimension, which is his domain, and the business dimension, which calls for the involvement of trained personnel to handle some of the day to day matters. Even Jesus appointed a treasurer to keep account of the funds that came in.

Failure to follow suitable accounting principles, including the appointment of a well trained administrator, may leave the ministry without necessary checks and balances that help to channel funds efficiently. Furthermore, it may bring the leader's integrity under serious question, whenever monies cannot be accounted for. One world renowned minister neglected to adhere to the system that had been put in place and fell in the wake of a major scandal, in which he was accused and convicted of converting millions of dollars of ministry funds for his own personal use. He spent quite a time in jail, reflecting on the errors of his ways.

> MINISTRY FUNDS FOR HIS OWN PERSONAL USE. HE SPENT QUITE A TIME IN JAIL, REFLECTING ON THE ERRORS OF HIS WAYS.

> When finances are flowing, go after projects that call for a
> **Heavy input of capital.**

There are numerous examples of ministries that failed to observe this simple principle. As a consequence, they missed golden opportunities to acquire property, to upgrade facilities and/or to greatly advance the pursuit of vision. Whether it was because of ignorance, misplaced priorities, disagreement, extreme caution or downright fear, the fact is that, in a season when multitudes passed through the doors of the sanctuary, leadership failed to capture the moment and maximize the possibilities that it presented.

Recently, a ministry, which showed irrefutable evidence of the fire of God burning in the midst, from the late 80's into the early 90's, celebrated over twenty-one years of operation. Sadly, it still rents the same facilities, at which it started, paying a ridiculous rate and with severe restrictions as to the types of activities permitted. What is more frustrating is the fact that just a few blocks away lies a plot of land, overgrown with grass and shrubbery, which it acquired in 1988, but on which it has so far failed to erect even a tent after all these years.

Lamentably, barring a major miracle, it does not seem as though the situation will change any time soon. The reasons for this are (1) the size of the present congregation is much smaller than what it used to be in the days of the fire. (2) The cash flow is not as liquid as it was then, when the congregation consisted of politicians, lawyers, magistrates, businessmen, doctors, just to mention a few. (3) The cost of the very facilities that were proposed for the site at that time, as evidenced by the plans on the walls and the model in the display case, has shot up from around $2m to over $10M, at today's prices.

What could have driven this ministry into its present predicament?

From my observations, at the top of the list are misplaced priorities. In its heyday, which, in reality; was its infancy, this ministry staged some mega conventions, at which all the speakers were high-profiled foreigners, whose demands included first class air travel, deluxe rooms in five star hotels for them and their entourage, ground transportation in luxury cars and exorbitant honorariums. This tallied into a major cost, which the ministry, in its infancy, was always hard pressed to pay. I remember being present at the closing ceremonies of many of these conventions and feeling pained in my heart, as the host pastor and, sometimes, one or more of the visiting speakers would literally beg the congregation to give towards paying off bills, totaling over $100,000.

In any season, to owe that amount at the end of a convention would raise serious questions about the prudence and wisdom of the pastor and his leaders in handling the finances of the ministry. One can only speculate what they could have accomplished, if they had not only cut back on the number of speakers, but also, invited those who were just as anointed but who would have made fewer demands. One thing for sure is that, even if they were not yet completed, today, the ministry would have been enjoying the use of its own premises, instead of paying an exorbitant rent for less than adequate facilities.

What are some of the lessons that we can learn from the experiences of this ministry?

- Set priorities right.
- Ownership of property and adequate facilities must always be at the top of the list.
- A large people-base usually translates into a large financial base—that is the ideal time to go after property acquisition and building construction.
- As long as a ministry is renting its facilities, it is still in the wilderness, since it is at the whims and fancies of the landlord. Make a decision not to die in the wilderness but to cross over into the Promised Land of property ownership.
- Within the first seven to ten years of its existence, a ministry should seek to acquire its first set of facilities, since that is

- a period when interest in the vision and enthusiasm for pursuing it are at their peak among the people.
- People are more inclined to give, when they see a project taking physical shape. Make a start, even if it is small.
- Have a current account for day to day expenses, but put the rest, designated for future use on several interest bearing accounts. It is not sinful for the church to seek to generate interest on its funds.
- If you cannot meet the demands of a minister whom you wish to invite to minister, then, you may not be ready for the level of ministry that he is offering.
- Since a convention is primarily for the benefit of the in-house congregation, in the lead up to it, the leader should challenge the people to plant seeds, so that all expenses, including the honorarium, would be already set aside before the opening night. Offerings accumulated during the meetings will then be a bonus, which could enhance the size of the honorarium and take care of unforeseen contingencies. It also will certainly eliminate the begging syndrome during the meetings.

Follow the laws of the land

A leader must become acquainted with and be prepared to follow the laws of the nation in which he operates, as it pertains to finances. He must be aware that, although, as a charitable organization, the ministry is exempt from paying taxes, he and others employed full-time by the ministry must pay taxes and other deductions on their wages to the relevant authorities. In a case cited earlier, of all the elements that worked together to precipitate the fall of the minister and the demise of the ministry, it was on the account of non-payment of taxes that the minister was sent to jail.

Teach on and demonstrate a positive attitude towards giving, prosperity and money

Traditionally, many pastors have been very apprehensive about mentioning the word 'prosperity' and more so, the word 'money', from the pulpit, except when trying to raise an offering. Yet, they expect the members of the congregation to pay their tithes, give offerings, make and pay pledges and plant seeds towards major projects. When this is not forthcoming, some are known to berate the people in the worst possible ways, labeling them as stingy and rebellious. Some have even dared to speak curses over God's people during fits of anger and frustration at falling revenues and having to default on monthly commitments.

What such pastors must understand is the fact that, like any other human endeavor, giving is a learned behavior. Consequently, in order to effect change and establish the practice of bountiful giving, the people must be taught on the biblical principles that pertain to the areas of giving, prosperity and money. One cannot assume that a person will come into church and automatically begin to give tithes and offerings on a consistent basis. For him to become a diligent giver, he has to be fed the correct information on the subject.

Now, granted that there are people who are bent on having their own way, anyway, where the problem lies, in the majority of cases, is in the attitude displayed by the pastor towards the subject. Since physical behavior is a manifestation of attitude that is rooted in the spirit, the pastor's attitude becomes the prevailing spirit in the congregation. If the pastor is hesitant to speak about money, then the people will be reluctant to give. If the pastor speaks against prosperity, then the people will live under a heavy cloud of guilt and condemnation, when in pursuit of a greater cash flow by way of increased income generating activities. If the pastor himself walks in poverty and always complains about lack, then the people will have grave problems in their finance People tend to follow their leader.

Therefore, in preparation for the increase in finances that naturally comes with an outpouring of the Spirit upon a people, the pastor must expose the people to systematic teaching on the subject. If he is not comfortable with doing it himself, then he must bring in other ministers who have a proven track record of, not just being sound teachers on the subject, but also, must be known for their giving, be visible in their prosperity and be experienced in the handling of money.

Such ministers may not necessarily be part of the fivefold ministry gifts nor should they necessarily have to come from outside of the congregation. They may be accountants, financial counselors, seasoned investors or successful business personnel, sitting right there among the people. Regardless of the source from which they come, though, as long as they carry that anointing, the wise pastor must tap into their expertise for his own benefit and that of the people.

Yet, the ultimate aim must be for the in-house leader to become the teacher, the demonstrator and the motivator of the people, when it comes to the pursuit of prosperity, the practice of giving and the acquisition and investment of money. When this becomes a reality, people will begin to experience upward mobility in their financial status and the church will see a steady increase in its cash flow. Even in this area, people learn by example.

Be honest about designated funds

Just as it is important for a leader not to misappropriate the funds of the ministry for his own use, so is it important for him not to redirect designated funds without informing the people. All too frequently we hear complaints from members of congregations about buildings that never got built or renovated although huge sums of money were raised for that purpose.

When a leader stands before a congregation to present the details of a proposed project and the plans for raising relevant funds, at least two things are at stake: his integrity and the general enthusiasm of the people. In many instances, all the people may not agree with the proposal, at first. However, they are usually won over by pastor's reasoning, his own passion for the project and, most importantly, by his excellent track record of always seeing a project through to the end.

As long as a pastor can repeat his performance in this instance and even show improvement by shortening time of delivery and cost effectiveness, then, he is guaranteed support for at least the project next in line. However, it is when people have put out the effort to raise the funds and time passes without the project even being started, let alone being finished, that the people feel let down and deceived.

What compounds the issue is when there is no communication from the pulpit on the issue as to whether plans have been changed, postponed or cancelled. This creates tension and raises questions of trust and truthfulness on the part of leadership. The tension heightens even more, if rumors begin to circulate about the funds having been redirected to some other project or used for paying bills. Worst of all is the case, where, at a later date, the pastor indicates that he is going after the same project, but will need more money because what was raised earlier is inadequate.

Such scenarios, as those painted above, are sure recipes for mistrust, withdrawal of enthusiasm and, in extreme cases, open rebellion, on the part of the congregation. You see, when a leader stands before the people to lay out the details of a project and calls for funding towards it, an unwritten but equally strong covenant is activated between him and the people. He offers them a rallying point around which they can commune with and challenge one another to excellence and draw meaning for their existence in the ministry and, in many cases, in their lives on the whole. In return, they offer him their skills, talents and support in pursuit of the vision for the ministry.

Consequently, when the leader does not deliver on the project within the proposed time frame or not at all, and does not have the courtesy to give an explanation that is both timely and feasible, he is in breach of covenant. Similar to what happens when a marriage breaks down, the people feel violated and disrespected. As a result, it becomes twice as difficult to stimulate their collective enthusiasm on the next occasion.

Yes, especially in a season when there is an outpouring of the Spirit in the Church, it is absolutely important that leaders of

God's people display honesty and openness concerning money. When monies are designated for a particular venture, it should be used as indicated. If for some unforeseen, unavoidable reason that designation has to be changed, a leader must come back to the people and inform them of that change.

The leader who would adopt such a practice is not only preserving his integrity and the spirit of unity in the congregation, but also, guarantees long life for the outpouring. Note that miracles, signs and wonders are the attractions to the outpouring, but it is integrity, truth and unity that keep it alive.

Let us bring this chapter to a close by citing a recent report posted on the internet, concerning the demise of the Brownsville Revival. It is written by a world renowned and well respected Christian journalist who is known for his honesty and frankness. If we examine it carefully, we should be able to identify within it, a great number of the pitfalls, which have been highlighted in Chapters Two and Three. My prayer is that all of us will take appropriate action to avoid a repeat of such a situation when the tsunami of God's glory hits our locale.

> What Happened to Brownsville's Fire? 6th June, 2006.
> By J. Lee Grady
>
> I'll never forget my first trip to Brownsville Assembly of God. It was 1995, the year an unusual spiritual eruption occurred at the monde script Pentecostal church in Pensacola, Fla.
>
> The rumor was that God had visited the quiet Southern town. I came not only as a reporter but also as a hungry seeker: In the early days of the revival, the faithful came by bus, car and airplane from all over the world. Eager worshipers waited for hours in the sweltering humidity to get a seat for 7 p.m. services that often lasted past mid night. When evangelist Steve Hill finished his nightly sermons, in which he demanded repentance from spiritual compromise, the majority of people in the auditorium

would run to the front of the church and bury their faces in the floor"

The Holy Spirit is easily quenched by pride, greed, selfish religious agendas and broken relationships." Wailing was commonly heard during those meetings. Some people shook under the weight of conviction. It did not matter if you were a drug addict needing conversion or a pastor living in secret sin, everyone found forgiveness and an unusual sense of refreshing in that holy place. My life was changed there. I wept in the car pet and repented for my journalistic cynicism. One night, in the midst of all the pandemonium near the stage, I ran over to where Hill was praying. He grabbed my head and screamed, "Fire! Fire! More, Lord!" I was one of the thousands who fell backward on that floor. I was not pretending. I felt as if God bad placed a heavy blanket of His presence on top of me. I don't question whether the Holy Spirit was in that place. But today, more than 10 years after the Pensacola Outpouring occurred, I am asking other questions. I am wondering why the church that hosted hundreds of thousands of visitors has shrunk to a few hundred members and now owes mil lions of dollars for a building they can't fill. I am struggling to understand why so many people who once were part of the Brownsville church now feel hurt and betrayed. I am wondering if the leaders of this movement mishandled the anointing of God's presence like Uzzah did when the ark of God almost toppled on the ground (see 2 Samuel 6:6–8). History shows us that revival is always risky. The devil opposes it, and carnal flesh gets in the way of it. The Holy Spirit is easily quenched by pride, greed, selfish religious agendas and broken relationships.

I can't be the judge of what brought Brownsville's demise. But we must face the facts and learn some lessons, or we will repeat the scenario next time.

It is no secret that relationships among various leaders at the Brownsville church were strained to the breaking point. Michael Brown, once the leader of the Brownsville Revival School of Ministry (BRSM), was fired in 2000 and then started his own training center that be eventually moved to North Carolina.

BRSM in its heyday had an enrollment of 1,200 students. That number shrank to 120 this year. This week the church announced that the ministry school will relocate to Louisiana, where it will be directed by revivalist Tommy Tenney.

"One of the lasting legacies of the Brownsville revival is the school," Tenney told me in an interview this week, noting that graduates are doing missionary work in 122 countries. One alumnus, in fact, was instrumental in discovering an unevangelized people group in Indonesia.

That is thrilling news. But my heart is still grieved that the church where this marvelous outpouring occurred is now a burned-out shell.

The pastor of the church during the revival, John Kilpatrick, resigned in 2003 and told parishioners he planned to remain at the church in an apostolic role. Kilpatrick installed Randy Feldschau as the new pastor; then this year Kilpatrick shocked the congregation by starting a new church in Daphne, Ala., 50 miles west of Pensacola.

Feldschau resigned a few months ago and moved to Texas, and Brownsville's attendance has dipped below 400. One former staff member told me that a large group of Brownsville members now attend a local Southern Baptist church in the city, while many others don't go anywhere. "People have been leaving for three or four years," the pastor told me. "Some are not in church at all, including some who were on staff. I don't know anyone who has not been hurt."

At one point during the heyday of the movement, Korean pastor David Yonggi Cho announced from Brownsville's pulpit that the revival "would last until Jesus comes." Certainly the fruit of this revival will remain that long. But for those in Pensacola who were swept up in the ecstasy of those early years, and then endured splits, resignations, debts and disappointments, the word "revival" now has a hollow ring to it.

Still, my heart cries: "Lord, do it again." Next time He does, I pray we will carry the ark the way God intended and keep our hands off of it. (7. Lee Grady is editor of Charisma and an award-winning journalist.) DISCLAIMER: Church of God and Faith News does not necessarily endorse or sanction all or any part of this news item.

"Sow to yourselves in righteousness, reap in mercy; break up your fallow ground for it is time to seek the Lord until he comes and rain righteousness upon you." (Hosea 10:12).

A Single Crop
Or A Perpetual Harvest -
The Choice Is Yours

Which would you prefer to have: A single bountiful crop or a perpetual harvest, which, although it may begin small, continues to increase both quantitatively and qualitatively as the years go by? This is no trick question. Yet, one must think carefully before giving an answer.

Just to sound noble, the majority of us may opt for the latter. Notwithstanding, it is the attitude and actions subsequent to the verbal declaration that would really reflect the true choice. May I run the risk of being accused of having an ultra-critical spirit by declaring that, based on my observation of human nature and behavior, the majority of us declare the latter with our mouth but live out the former, in reality?

You may not be as disposed to level your guns at me, if you take an honest look at the many people who line up every day in the lotto lines or who complain ever so often of being duped by some get rich-quick scheme. They hang their fortunes on one big windfall and hardly see much value in the old adage—'Hard work brings great rewards.' Needless to say, only a few ever come into such a windfall and. even then, many soon lose it because of not being mentally or otherwise prepared to handle it.

No doubt, you may be questioning the relevance of this analogy to the present discourse. Bear with me a while and I will show you its undeniable significance to the overall development of a code of behavior for this prophetic cycle that we have entered.

Very disturbingly, the above scenario is played out, in principle, in the Church, time after time, as it pertains to the move of God among us. Many ministers have primed their congregations to wait on that 'big bang'—that day when suddenly people begin to walk out of wheelchairs or some supernatural occurrence takes place during a worship service—before they proclaim that there is a move of God, taking place in their midst. In the process, they do not attach much value to the times when, after many years of intercession by a wife, her husband is finally at the altar crying out to God for salvation. Even the occasions when people who had been hurting for years finally get their healing by forgiving their abusers go largely unnoticed. If they had seen these seemingly insignificant occurrences as signals of God's intent to do a new thing in their midst, then these ministers would have taken the congregation before God to inquire after His heart for the ministry. The result could have been that a little spark might have set the forest on fire.

I will be the first to admit that there are those who have actually experienced the 'big bang' from time to time in their ministries. However, in a great many instances, owing to inadequate spiritual and psychological preparedness, it has remained just that-a loud noise that was. Others have tried to recreate it in every service since that first explosion, but, instead of going before God for fresh fire, they have employed their own methods. All they have managed to achieve for all their efforts, however, has been nothing louder than the sound of firecrackers in a New Year's Eve celebration.

Do you know that God is well aware of this quirk of human nature? After all, it is He who made us. Let me inform you, then, that since He is aware of it, He has established counter measures to deal with it, in His Word. Based upon what the Lord has been revealing to me, Hosea 10:12 provide the most powerful antidotes against this weakness in the Body of Christ. Consequently, we will dedicate the next few pages to an analysis of this verse with a view to extracting the life saving serum that we so desperately need in the Body of Christ at this time. The text reads:

> *Sow for yourselves according to righteousness (uprightness and right standing with God); reap according to mercy and loving-kindness. Break up your uncultivated ground, for it is time to seek the Lord, to inquire for and of Him, and to require His favor, till He comes and teaches you righteousness and rains His righteous gift of salvation upon you (Hosea 10:12, AMP).*

For quite some years, this verse of scripture has carried special significance for me. When the Lord laid the mantle of the Prophet upon me in 1986, it was as much a surprise to me as it was to others who knew me in the music ministry. The Lord completely defied the accepted norms and traditions followed by the denomination in which I grew up and to which I was an ardent adherent, at the time. He did not ask anyone's permission, not even mine, to anoint and appoint me to the office of the Prophet. He was guided solely by His own methodology, as recorded in Isaiah 55:8, AMP, 'For My thoughts are not your thoughts, neither are your ways my ways, says the Lord.' Looking back, now, I thank Him, so much, that He never surrenders His sovereignty.

Immediately as the mantle of the Prophet rested upon me, there was a distinct shift in the way people began to relate to me. Many acknowledged, without question, that the choice was the Lord's doing and fully supported me. They pledged to cover me in prayer, which most have been doing faithfully, since then. On the other hand, there were those who knew and acknowledged that it was the Lord's doing but could not reconcile with the question of why God had chosen me and not someone else. However, there was also a great company of those who did not think that God had anything to do with it at all. They speculated that I had either become too full of myself or that some demon from the deepest abyss of hell had suddenly taken possession of my soul. As such, they did not hold out much hope for me getting very far or lasting too long with this 'prophetic foolishness', as some labeled it.

Notwithstanding, I was convinced, beyond a shadow of a doubt, that it was the Lord who had moved by His sovereign will in my life. You see, left to me alone, preaching the gospel and more so, doing it as a Prophet, was the furthest thing from my mind. I had seen enough things for which I could not get suitable answers, while growing up as a pastor's son, to convince me of that.

However, throughout those dark days of persecution and isolation, I made up my mind that the predictions of the gainsayers would not be fulfilled in my life. Consequently, I became desperate in my search for answers from the Lord. The main concern I would consistently place before the Lord was, "Lord, would it be your intention to initiate such a radical move in my life and then have it die in a short time? If it is not so, then instruct me how to make it last." To this the Lord replied by not only showing me how to make it last, but also, how to have it gather momentum and magnitude, as the years go by. Now, twenty-one years later (as I write, at the beginning of 2007), the testimonies of thousands of mended lives across the earth are proof positive that it works.

In guiding me through the maze that is the prophetic ministry, the Lord has used Hosea 10:12 as a compass, par excellence, to plot my course. Even now, as we enter this prophetic cycle of the Outpouring, He is exposing me to a greater level of revelation flowing out of it. I am sharing them with you with the intention of stimulating you to passionately seek the face of the Lord for the principles that will help you maintain the anointing that you will receive: an anointing that is custom-made to your specific calling or that of the ministry to which you belong.

The first angle from which we will examine this Verse exposes to us the foundation upon which it is constructed. Hosea uses an agriculture-based analogy, which is borne out by expressions such as sow, reap and fallow ground. In so doing, he profiles the disposition of a true farmer.

A true farmer does not go into the field with one harvest in mind. After the first cycle of sowing and reaping, he does not close up shop. Instead, the last harvest motivates him to go back into the field, plow up the ground again and sow more seeds, expecting an even more bountiful harvest this time around.

On the spiritual plane, God inspires Hosea to focus on this disposition and task of the natural farmer to highlight the composite question, which we asked at the beginning of this chapter: 'Which would you prefer to have? A single bountiful crop or a perpetual harvest, which continues to increase both quantitatively and qualitatively as the years go by, although it may begin small?' In pursuit of answers, in this context, we will reword it to read, 'which do you prefer - a one-cycle move of God or an ever-increasing, perpetual outpouring of His anointing?'

If you take the first option, then, all you will experience is a REVIVAL and the rest of this discourse may be of no help to you at all. However, if you choose the second option, then read on. Note, though, that you are in for an infusion of divine rev elation into your life like you have never experienced before. You may very well be hard pressed to find room to contain it by dint of its volume, depth and intensity. I implore you, therefore, MAKE ROOM FOR THE OUTPOURING.

However, the onus is upon you to fill the prescription to the letter. Let us explore the verse, in focus, by breaking it into segments. We will use the King James Version, with cross references to the Amplified and other versions, as we go along.

Sow to yourselves in righteousness

There are two pre-requisites for sowing. One obliges the sower to locate the seed for sowing and the other saddles him with the responsibility of preparing the ground for receiving the seed. Since we are dealing with spiritual matters, here, the task is then to define both the terms 'ground' and 'seed' in their spiritual dimensions. Neither task should be too difficult, though.

If we consider that the instruction is to sow to ourselves, then, the ground for sowing has to be our inner man. Our inner man constitutes our soul and our spirit. Our spirit is the image of God within us. It is always willing to please God. However, in the majority of cases, the scope of its influence upon our lives is determined and sometimes short-circuited by the negative control of our soul. Jesus was fully aware of this dilemma of the human being and cautioned his disciples accordingly, "The spirit indeed is willing, but the flesh (human nature or soul) is weak." (Matthew 26:41, AMP).

Consequently, the true task at hand, in preparing our inner man for sowing, is the plowing up of our soul. Our soul houses our mind, intellect, will, attitude and desires, among other elements. It means, then, that in the process of preparing our souls to receive the seeds of righteousness, intellectual rationalization must give way to faith; our will must submit to God's will; our attitude must go through progressive, positive adjustments; our desires must be purified and our minds must be renewed.

To fully accomplish this task, we must construct a plow, sufficiently powerful and efficient to do the job. The main components of this plow are repentance, forgiveness, introspection, and deep soul searching powered by an engine, running on fuel that is enriched by prayer, fasting, praise, worship, meditation and obedience.

When such a plow is skillfully driven across the landscape of our inner man, every furrow that it makes will turn up some alarming elements, which we need to cart away. Prominent among them would most likely be anger, wrath, malice, hatred, un-forgiveness, rebellion, disobedience, lust and pride. In short, the plowing up of the inner man is the same as the putting off of the old man (Colossians 3:8); the mortifying of our flesh (Colossians 3:5-7) and the renewing of the spirit of our minds (Ephesians 4:23) that Apostle Paul recommends to the Church.

Additionally, the plowing up of the inner man, in preparation for sowing, must be aligned to the principles espoused by Jesus in the parable of the sower and the seed in Matthew 13. In that parable, Jesus identifies the four types of soils that a sower encounters in any one season of sowing. He relates each type of soil to a particular temperament with which people approach the teaching of the word of God, which he calls seed. (Mark 4:11). According to Jesus, the four types of soil are wayside soil, stony ground, thorny soil and good soil.

Jesus equates the wayside soil to people who hear the word of God but, because of ignorance, never experience a change in attitude and behavior. He describes those who initially receive the word with joy but later become offended, when persecuted because of it, as having the disposition of stony ground. People who hear the word but allow the 'cares of this world and the deceitfulness of riches' to render them unfruitful are classified as soil overrun by thorns. Finally, Jesus categorizes those who bear fruit or make the necessary adjustments in response to the word that they hear, as having a good-soil mentality.

Based on the above, then, the task of plowing up the inner man becomes even graver. On the one hand, we are now responsible for ascertaining what type of soil we are, while, on the other level, having discovered so, we must now commit ourselves to digging up our souls and removing all impurities until wayside soil, stony ground and thorn-infested land become good soil. This we must do, regardless of how long it takes or how painful it may be. We do not want to be guilty of being only hearers of the word. We want to be doers, as well.

As soon as the plowing up of the inner man is done, the sowing must begin. The admonition is to sow 'in righteousness' so the seeds for this task must be the Word of God. It means that we are being called upon to develop a new passion and hunger for searching, memorizing, meditating on and living out the scriptures.

Yet, we must not interpret this as a challenge to see how many chapters we can read in a day or even whether we can read the entire Bible in a year. Neither of these exercises will truly provide seed with the level of potency to produce the quantity and quality of harvest that we really need in this season. In going to the scriptures to obtain seeds of righteousness for sowing in the inner man, our approach cannot be with any less intensity than what David or Paul recommends.

David's approach, as recorded in Psalms 1, is to condition himself into delighting in the law of God-causing his eyes to light up with excitement and his adrenaline to pump vigorously—whenever he hears or reads it. Note carefully that David specifies the law of the Lord as distinct from the word of the Lord. You see, his passion is not so much to find another promise from God, but more so to familiarize himself with the principles of God that will help him to order his steps and inculcate discipline into his life. His pledge is that, having located such laws, he will meditate on them day and night.

It is important to note that for David and certainly for us, meditation is not necessarily the emptying of the mind, as practiced by the devotees of eastern religions. Such a practice is extremely dangerous and may lead to demonic possession. Rather, he sees his mind as a processing plant into which he receives the word, mulls over it, breaks it apart, searches for references and sets up linkages, until he extracts the power for living from that word.

The intensity of this exercise is even more marked, when one sees the process as akin to working out in a gym. For every muscle we intend to tone, the instructor orders us to do a specific amount of 'reps' or repeated exercises until we achieve our goal. Such is the act of meditating upon the word of God. We have to take up that Bible over and over like weights; commit verses to memory like running the treadmill, and continuously repeat them like jumping to music on the aerobics floor. The major difference is that instead of strengthening the biceps and triceps, we fortify the concepts and the precepts by which we walk before God.

Apostle Paul uses a different analogy but conveys the same message and with just as much intensity. He sees the acquisition of seeds of righteousness similar to a student's quest for knowledge. In 2 Timothy 2:15, he admonishes his young protégé, Timothy, to "Study to show yourself approved unto God, a workman that need not to be ashamed, rightly dividing the word of truth."

Here, Paul is advising both Timothy and by extension, the Church, that the secret to accessing God's reservoir of revelation is to take on the searching of the scriptures with the same diligence and dedication as that of a student pursuing his studies It means, then, that if a student has to make time for studying at the expense of other pleasures, we too must make the sacrifice of setting aside time to study God's word.

Additionally, since every student acquires knowledge with examination and certification in mind, we too must prepare ourselves to be tested on what we learn. Every student knows how ashamed he would feel if he fails, so he strives to be successful in all his examinations. Even so, we too should seek to give intelligent answers, both in word and deed, to any man who questions us about the word of God that we have embraced.

In spite of being cramped for space, we will allow ourselves the luxury of citing one more scripture on this theme. It forms an integral part of the steps to success that Joshua receives from God, at the very beginning of his tenure as leader of Israel. We would do well to take heed to it, as we seek to secure seeds of righteousness for sowing in our inner man. It is really self-explanatory:

> *This book of the Law shall not depart out of your mouth, but you shall meditate on it day and night, that you may observe and do according to all that is written in it; for then you shall make your way prosperous, and then you shall deal wisely and have good success (Joshua 1:8, AMP).*

It is only fitting, then, that I should short list some key passages of scripture that have become veritable seedpods for me, in my own search for seeds of righteousness. They are some of the richest deposits of seeds of righteousness that you may find in the word of God. The aim is to jump-start you into a search of your own.

Repentance—Psalms 51; 2 Peter 3:9; Luke 13:3&5.

Resistance against sin—Psalms 119:11; James 4:7&17.

Forgiveness—John 21; Matthew 18; Mark 11:25.

Peace—Isaiah 26:3; Psalms 42; John 14:27.

Testing and Trials—Psalms 23;

Romans 8:28; 1 Peter 4:12–19.

Giving—Exodus 35; Malachi 3; Luke 6:38.

Thanks giving, Praise, and Worship Psalms 100; Psalms 29; John 4:21–24. Renewing the Mind-Romans 12; Proverbs 4; Ephesians 4:23.

Spiritual Warfare—Psalms 18; Psalms 37; Ephesians 6.

Having obtained our supply of seeds of righteousness and having ploughed up our inner man, we must take care as to how we do the actual sowing. The simplest way to grasp this is to conjure up in our minds a picture of a farmer sowing his field in Bible times. The farmer would either tie an apron around his waist or hold a basket in one hand. He would fill either of these with seeds as he set out on a walk across his already ploughed up field. As he went. He would take handfuls of seed and broadcast them generously in a wide arc in front of him. Sometimes he would be very contemplative as he did so, but at other times a farmer would actually sing Psalms and other songs as he went along. Whichever was the farmer's preference, to the on looker; he always seemed to be doing his work to a rhythm.

Herein, therefore, lies the whole principle of sowing seeds of righteousness. Since these seeds of righteousness are actually principles from the Word of God and the field is our inner man, there are times when sowing would demand that we quietly con template or meditate on the scriptures. This serves to etch them indelibly upon the fleshy tablets of our hearts and bury them deep inside our memory for instant recall at a later time. At other times, we will have to use our mouths as a launching pad and speak the scriptures all day long, so that our own ears can hear them and register them in our minds.

Moreover, we may have to follow the advice of both Prophet Isaiah and Apostle Paul and sing the word of God. Isaiah admonishes us in Isaiah 54:1, "Sing O barren, thou that didst not bear; break forth into singing and cry aloud." In much the same vein, Paul's recommendation in Ephesians 5:19 is, "Speaking to yourselves in

Psalms and hymns and spiritual songs, singing and making melody in your heart to God."

When we lift our hands or dance, in praise and worship, or use our feet to symbolize the action of a soldier in battle as we do spiritual warfare, it is similar to that of the farmer rhythmically broadcasting his seeds across his field and burying them deep in the soil as he walks over them.

When all of these activities are under girded with prayer, fasting and unfeigned obedience, we manage to establish the following important principles. It is as though we are setting up scarecrows at strategic points in the field to keep the birds from eating our seed. It also mirrors the action of weeding the seed lings, on a daily basis, to keep the thorns and thistles away. Additionally prayer, fasting and uncompromising obedience work together with praise and worship to water the seeds until they germinate into seedlings and the seedlings become trees that 'bring forth fruit in their season.' (Psalms 1:3).

Reap in mercy

Genesis 8:22, KJV reads, "While the earth remaineth, seedtime and harvest, and cold and heat and summer and winter, and day and night shall not cease." This verse is a segment of the edict that God issued, in the process of restoring the earth's rhythm after it had been knocked out of sync by Adam's fall from grace. God puts the earth on a set of irreversible, synchronized cycles. At the top of the list is the cycle of sowing and reaping, which is directly related to this stage of our discourse.

The term, 'seedtime', presupposes that present in the environment, are all the requirements and conditions that encourage and sustain the germination, development and maturation of a seed, into a fruit bearing tree. Among these are the following:

- viable seeds
- well prepared, fertile soil
- favorable weather conditions

- constant vigilance against intruders.
- a pledge to be diligent at the task of caring for the crop.

As long as all these factors are working together, there comes a point when seedtime gives way to harvest time. Harvest time is the period in which the trees that grew out of the seeds are laden with fruit.

The nature of the fruit and the volume of the harvest are each governed by separate natural laws that lend credence to biblical principles. For example, one should not expect to see fruit different in nature from the seed that one has sown because 'A man reaps only what he sows.' (Galatians 6:7, NIV). Similarly, the size of the harvest usually reflects the volume of seeds sown because 'Whoever sows sparingly will reap sparingly, whoever sows generously will also reap generously.' (2 Corinthians 9:6, NIV). It stands to reason, then, that the sower holds the major key to the quality and quantity of harvest that he receives.

Taking all of the above elements into consideration, let us now explore the implications of the statement 'reap in mercy.' As mentioned previously, Hosea seems to have had a sound knowledge of agriculture. Consequently, in rendering this prophetic admonition, he incorporates the full cycle of agriculture's most fundamental principle-sowing and reaping-in an analogy that clearly elucidates God's response to His people's hunger for righteousness. In so doing, Hosea alerts us to the fact that if we sow seeds of righteousness then we should expect to reap a harvest of mercy. This is exactly what Jesus teaches us in Matthew 5:6, when he announces that all who hunger and thirst after righteousness will be filled with or reap a harvest of the very righteousness which they seek.

At first glance, one may think that there is some measure of contradiction, here, in that the expected harvest from the seeds of righteousness is not righteousness but mercy. However, this is not so. Mercy and righteousness are one and the same. They are both elements of a much larger cluster called the 'fruit of the Spirit, as recorded in Galatians 5:22.

Therefore, when we sow seeds of righteousness, what we really reap is the full assortment of the fruit of the Spirit.

The term, 'fruit of the Spirit', first appears in Galatians 5:22. It basically refers to the godly character that should define the life of anyone who claims to be a child of God. In that verse, Apostle Paul itemizes the elements that make up the cluster as love, joy, peace, longsuffering, gentleness, goodness, faith, meekness and temperance. However, such a list is not cast in concrete. It is simply representative of a more exhaustive compilation of the attributes of godly character recorded throughout the scriptures.

One simply has to go to the dictionary or thesaurus in search of synonyms for each element of the cluster and one will realize how fathomless a reservoir the fruit of the Spirit can be. This is what constitutes the harvest that one enjoys whenever one sets about making changes within the inner man, as directed by the Holy Spirit.

David makes the said changes and testifies, in Psalms 1, that he has developed such a delight for the word of God that he is now meditating upon it or sowing it into his inner man and diligently watering it, day and night. The benefits are so noteworthy that the only analogy of he can think of, in his attempt to adequately describe himself, is that of an evergreen tree planted by the rivers of water that bears fruit, when it is supposed to. In practical terms, David's life has been transformed from instability to stability, from barrenness to fruitfulness, from failure to success and from poverty to prosperity.

In both Psalms 27 and Psalms 84, David talks of his passion for the presence of God as denoted by his longing to be in the house of God. It is apparent that he did make the necessary adjustments to his time table to cater to the demands of this passion because, in Psalms 92:13&14, KJV, he testifies of the harvest of benefits that has come his way. He declares, "Those that be planted in the house of the Lord shall flourish in the courts of the Lord. They shall still bring forth fruit in old age; they shall be fat and flourishing."

Proverbs 3 also bears record of the sowing and reaping principle. In verse one, God admonishes Solomon to obey His word. In verse three, He exhorts Solomon to shut out all hatred, selfishness, hypocrisy and falsehood from his heart and, in their place, create a passion for truth. Verses two and four celebrate the expected benefits or harvest that accrues to Solomon. They are a long life that is worth living, peace, favour, good understanding, and high-esteem in the sight of God and man.

The sowing and reaping principle is also at work in Joshua 1. In verses 3&4, the Lord promises Joshua a harvest of material possessions: 'every place upon which the sole of your foot shall tread, that I have given you.' In verse 5, it is a harvest of invincibility: No man shall be able to stand before thee all the days of thy life... 'a harvest of divine protection and guidance—'As I was with Moses, so shall I be with you..., and of divine presence and constancy—'I will not fail you nor forsake you.' In verse 8, it is one of fulfilled destiny: 'For then you shall make your way prosperous, and then you shall deal wisely and have good success.' (Joshua 1:8, AMP).

However, we must take careful note of the fact that all of these promises hinge upon Joshua's willingness to make the necessary changes within his inner man. He has to plow up the inside and remove every stumbling block of apprehension and every parasitic vine of discouragement. In place of those negative elements, he must 'Be strong, confident and of good courage.' (Joshua 1:6, KJV).

The next step calls for Joshua to sow the word of God into his life by meditating upon it day and night, until it springs forth into a walk of obedience, in accordance with the will of God. God's instruction to Joshua are, "This book of the law shall not depart out of your mouth, but you shall meditate upon it day and night, that you may observe and de according to all that is written in it..."

One can never engage in any meaningful discussion on sowing and reaping, in scripture, and not, of necessity, also touch on the question of giving and receiving money and/or other material goods. Anyone who sets out to plow up his soul, in preparation for a new move of God in his life, has to bring his attitude towards tithes and offerings in line with God's Word. One cannot claim genuine repentance (change of mind and direction) or to be fully anointed, unless there is surrender in this area as well. The truth is that disobedience of the tithes and offering principle incurs the wrath of God, which imposes a curse upon all areas of endeavor, subsequent to every violation on the part of the individual.

Through Malachi, God reprimands Israel for robbing Him. Completely bewildered upon hearing such an indictment, they wonder how that can be possible. To this the Lord replies, "You have withheld your tithes and offerings." (Malachi 3:8). Malachi goes on to state that as a result of such an act of banditry, the nation has lived under a curse, which has opened the gates for devourers to devastate the land.

However, God, being the merciful and benevolent One that He is, even in judgment, offers Israel a remedy for reversing the curse. It rests upon the willingness of the entire nation, individually and corporately, to sow seeds of righteousness and obedience by bringing 'all the tithes into the storehouse'. (Malachi 3:10). If they only obey, the intended harvest of mercy will far exceed the magnitude and time span of their needs:

> *I will open you the windows of heaven, and pour you out a blessing, that there would not be room enough to receive it. And I will rebuke the devourer for your sakes, and he would not destroy the fruits of your ground. (Malachi 3:10&11).*

Jesus comes along, many years later, and endorses the principle of giving and receiving (sowing and reaping), when he declares in Luke 6:38, "Give and it shall be given unto you, good measure pressed down, and shaken together, and running over shall men give into your bosom." He then goes a step further and attaches an addendum towards the end of the verse that directly addresses the attitude with which one should give or sow, "…For with the mea sure you deal out (give) it will be measured back to you."

In his turn, Apostle Paul amplifies upon Jesus' thoughts, when, in writing his second letter to the Church at Corinth, he admonishes them and by association, us, today:

> *(Remember) this: he who sows sparingly and grudgingly will also reap sparingly and grudgingly, and he who sows generously will also reap generously and with blessings. Let each one (give) as he has made up his own mind and*

purposed in his heart, not reluctantly or sorrowfully or under compulsion, for God loves a cheerful (joyous, prompt-to-do-it) giver-whose heart is in his giving (2 Corinthians 9:6&7, AMP).

In this verse, Apostle Paul highlights the sowing and reaping principle as being fail-proof. However, he, too, lets it be known that the quality and quantity of the harvest are heavily dependent on the attitude with which the sower sows.

As we close this segment, let us take an in-depth look at Psalms 24, as it pertains to the law of sowing and reaping in this season of the outpouring. As I awoke one morning, the Lord led me to base my prayer session on the verses of this chapter. In the process, He showed me the simple but powerful premise upon which this Psalms is built.

In the first two verses, David gives an all-inclusive assessment of the vastness of the Lord's resources, both material and human: "The earth is the Lord's, and everything in it, the world and all who live in it." (Psalms 24:1&2, NIV). What David does not say but clearly implies, though, is that all that God possesses is available to us, His people. It is quite clear that David, himself has tapped into and has been drawing heavily from that treasure trove of wealth. Not being selfish, he is now delivering an invitation to all and sundry to come and get ours.

In verses 3&4, David lays down both a challenge and an advisory wrapped in one: Get interested in acquiring your share but be careful to observe the rules of acquisition. These rules of acquisition are a veritable checklist for preparing the landscape of the inner man to receive seeds of righteousness. 'He who has clean hands and a pure heart'—all that we do and the motive for doing it must be pleasing to God. Who hath not lifted up his soul unto vanity, nor sworn deceitfully'—we must align our passions and desires to the will of God and be willing to fulfill the pledges that we make.

The rest of the chapter outlines the dimensions of the harvest that accrue to those who satisfy the stated conditions. Verse 5 declares blessings or profits, both natural and spiritual, together with the gift of salvation-'He (who ploughs up his inner man and sows the seeds of righteousness) shall receive the blessing from the Lord, and righteousness from the God of his salvation.' Verse 6 promises the breaking of generation curses and the establishment of a lineage of covenant keepers, in much the same vein as Abraham, Isaac and Jacob. Verses 7–10 outline ascendancy into a new realm of authority with which to bring the spirit world into order. Such is the extent to which God is covenanted to shower blessings upon those who are willing to comply with His will.

Again, time and space will not allow us to proceed any further in highlighting the myriad of examples that testify to the unfailing principle of sowing and reaping. However, we can safely cover everything on the subject by venturing an expanded rendering of Hosea 10:12a. 'Sow to yourself in righteousness, reap in mercy,' may then read, 'Do whatever it takes to align your spirit, soul and body to the principles of righteousness and you will be sure to see both spiritual fruits and natural blessings abound in your life.'

Yet, as bountiful as this harvest of mercy—spiritual fruits and natural blessings—may appear, it only represents one season of sowing and reaping. This prompts us to return to the question that we set out to explore in this section. Which do you prefer-a REVIVAL, which is nothing but a one-cycle move of God, or do you wish to experience a perpetual, ever increasing release of the Spirit of God, which the scripture calls the OUTPOURING? As explained earlier, many verbally declare the latter but live the former, in reality.

There are three main reasons why an individual or ministry may settle for a revival instead of going after the outpouring. The first may be likened unto the disposition and behavior of a casual gardener. He simply plants for fun and, at some time and by sheer fortune, he may happen upon a big harvest. However, since he cannot tell what he did to obtain it, he is wary of going back to the field, lest he fails to produce the same results the next time around. Consequently, counting himself rather fortunate to have done so, he chooses to reap the harvest and enjoy the fruits, while they last.

Similarly, an individual or ministry that operates on the fringes of Kingdom life, i.e. it is more concerned about doctrinal accuracy than having an ever-intensifying passion for the heart and mind of God, may from time to time stumble upon a powerful release of God's glory. This may come as a result of some itinerant evangelist or prophet conducting a series of meetings in the assembly.

I usually label this phenomenon a Suitcase Revival. The visiting minister comes in and ignites a fire. For as long as he is there, the fire burns on, but, when he leaves, he seems to pack away more than his clothes in his suitcase. He seems to also take away the fire with him. There is no continuity, because the resident pastor sees the anointing as being vested in the visitor and does not think that he, too, can flow in such a dimension. Depending on the intensity of the anointing fire with which this prophet or evangelist ministers, the individual or assembly may run on the momentum that he leaves behind for quite some time. However, if prior to the meetings, there is no proper ploughing up of the inner man, both individually and corporately, the momentum soon wanes and the fire goes out. Steep ignorance of the heart of God for the ministry further compounds the issue to precipitate such an occurrence. Is this what you want for yourself or your ministry, or are you looking for something much deeper and longer lasting?

An individual or ministry may also get stuck in the one-cycle revival syndrome, even when all the pre-requisite preparations are made. This may result from the work of a pair of spirits cited much earlier. They are pride and complacency.

Pride generates a sense of achievement. It causes people to see the release of spiritual gifts coming mainly by way of human effort, marginalizing the sovereign will of God, in the process. It also makes a congregation feel that it has arrived and as such is better than any other.

Complacency, on the other hand, gets one caught up in the ecstasy of the harvest to the extent of erroneously thinking that it will always be so. There is no vigilance on the part of the leader and congregation, to continuously check the pulse of the movement and the temperature of the fire to as certain its vitality and to make the necessary adjustments for keeping it alive.

When these two spirits work in tandem, they lead entire ministries to miss and even discredit subsequent moves of God by taking the present harvest into the storehouse and locking the doors against the inflow of anything new. It has been said that, generally, the heaviest critics of the present move of God, in the main, come from among those who were major players in the last move, and who, sadly, are still stuck there. How lamentable!

The third reason for many people not going beyond revival steins from an unwillingness to continue paying the price for ploughing up the inner man. They consider converting pleasure time into time for seeking God, the breaking of unprofitable relationships in favor of establishing intimacy with God and the denial of ungodly passions, as being a price too high to pay. It is as though the devil blinds their eyes from seeing the great leap forward that their lives have taken, during the period before and since the outbreak of Holy Ghost fire. Instead, just like the experience of Israel in the wilderness, there is a rekindling of a yearning for the onions and garlic of Egypt—the beggarly elements of the era in which the old man ruled (Colossians 3).

What all three categories of people fail to recognize is the unfailing truth of a vital principle of life, which we cited earlier- Whatever we obtain, we must maintain if we desire to retain it. Wherever people ignore this principle, another law, called the Law of Diminishing Returns, brings death-yielding pressure to bear upon the situation.

It is an irrefutable truth that, in spite of how large a harvest may be in the natural, it is not inexhaustible. If one draws from its resources, without replenishing it, it will soon be depleted. In the same vein, even if the entire harvest is left untouched in a warehouse, its quantity and quality will still diminish because of deterioration over time and will eventually prove to be unprofitable to the farmer.

In principle, it is the same with the spiritual harvest. If one does not continue to observe the principles and practices that brought it on in the first place, the movement will soon lose momentum and the fire will certainly die, regardless of the initial intensity with which it came. The mournful cries of so many individuals and ministries for God to rekindle the fires of now defunct movements are evidence enough that this is an undeniable truth.

In light of the above, what, then, should be our disposition, when a move of God explodes within our lives, individually and corporately? Hosea does provide the answer, as he continues his prophetic declaration in Hosea 10:12.

Break up your fallow ground

The term 'fallow ground' generally refers to soil that is untilled. However, in the context of our discussion, it carries an additional dimension of meaning. It describes ground that once produced a harvest, but now lies uncultivated. The question that arises here most naturally is, 'Why does it now lie in this condition?'

It is quite possible that the plot of ground has been abandoned because the farmer has reaped the harvest and has absolutely no intention of planting again. It is also possible that he is so caught up in the euphoria of the last harvest that he cannot find time to go back to work in the field. A third possibility may be that some serious matter has arisen in the farmer's life, since the last harvest. It has drawn so much on his resources that it has rendered him incapable of continuing his trade.

Regardless of the reason, though, if this piece of ground remains fallow for too long, the elements of nature can take heavy toll upon its ability to sustain growth and produce a bountiful harvest in the future. The sun can cause bleaching, making its surface as hard as concrete and rendering it unfriendly to seed. The rain can lead to leeching, causing the topsoil to run off with all its nutrients. The combined effect of the sun and the rain can lead to dusty conditions which may allow the wind to blow the loose soil away.

However, there is another prospect, which should excite those who have genuinely identified with the latter part of the question in focus. It is possible that the ground may be fallow but only for a little while longer. The farmer, having a clear understanding of times and seasons, is just about to put his plow to the soil one more time, so as to activate another cycle of sowing and reaping.

Such a farmer is not a hobbyist but a professional. He sees farming, not as what one does in one's spare time, but as his life's calling. He truly understands the principles of farming. He knows that genuine profitability in his calling does not come to one who settles just for a single season of sowing and reaping. It only comes to the one who continues to follow the related processes: ploughing up the soil, sowing the seeds, planting the seedlings, tending to the plants and reaping the fruits from one season to another. That's the one who is in for the long haul and not just for some overnight thrill.

Herein, then, lies the full spiritual implication of Hosea's admonition to 'Break up your fallow ground.' Hosea blows a trumpet from the top of the mountains to us all, 'Develop the disposition of a true farmer. Understand your times and seasons. Don't you settle for just a revival i.e. a one-cycle move of God! You will only realize and increase the true value of your sacrifice as you continue to plough up and seed your inner man. It's only in this way that you will be correctly positioned to move from glory to glory, in the rhythm, which God has set for you.'

For it is time to seek the Lord

A clear understanding of times and seasons is an absolute prerequisite for sensitizing us to the next move of God. This is noteworthy since the next move may come even when we are still caught up in the swirling tides of the current one.

As indicated in a previous segment entitled, 'Prophetic Sequencing', God revealed Himself to Ezekiel as a wheel in the middle of a wheel. This mirrors a picture of the creation of ripples, when a stone is thrown into a pool. There is a rapid emergence of concentric circles of water, chasing one another to the edge of the pool. In so doing, God showed to Ezekiel and to us, by extension, the process by which He releases His prophetic anointing and imposes His sovereign will upon the earth.

It means, then, that all the moves of God are inter-related. The truth is that, as long as we are willing to go along with God, it really becomes one move, developing in phases along a continuum that ultimately leads us to reflect the image and glory of God. Each new phase draws its initial energy from the one that went before, until it can create a momentum and character of its own. Therefore, it behooves the movers and shakers of the present move to acknowledge what went before, maximize the present and be ready, not only to help usher in the next move, but also, to be mentally and spiritually prepared to make the transition into it.

However, I must hasten to say that although we may safely forecast that God will move, it is highly risky to try to predict, with any degree of accuracy, when and in what the move form will be. Even a cursory glance at how Israel chased the cloud of God's glory, in the wilderness will be very instructive, here: When the cloud moved Israel moved; but when the cloud stayed Israel stayed.' (Exodus 40). Note well, though, that there was no specific time frame within which the moving of the cloud occurred. It could be a year after the last move or as early as the morning after. It meant that Israel had to remain alert with their eyes on the cloud and quick in their response to its moving

In principle, this is still the nature of God's glory, today—not even the most accurate prophet can tell exactly where God will go next. Therefore, it is incumbent upon all who intend to pursue God to seek Him continuously, concerning what is the next item on His agenda. It is what will keep us in step with His rhythm and save us from the embarrassment and frustration of being stuck in a place where God used to be—the worst place that an individual or ministry can find itself.

Undoubtedly, Hosea governed his walk with God along these guidelines. This explains why he would incorporate the exhortation, 'for it is time to seek the Lord', as part of his admonition for us to go beyond revival—a one cycle move of God.

We now need to explore why it is so critical to seek the Lord continuously, as regards the release of His anointing fire, even when we are still moving along on the swirling currents of the present move. Here are the reasons:

- The glory that marks a move of God belongs to Him and Him alone. The anointing that ignites and sustains the fire belongs to God.
- The nature, scope and direction of every move are in God's hands.
- No two moves are exactly the same, even though they may be taking place among the same people and in the same place.
- Continuously seeking God's face stimulates a fresh flow of revelation and anointing that saves us from having the need to duplicate, in our locale, what we see in another place.
- God is the owner and dispenser of both the seeds of righteousness and the rain of righteousness that nourishes and ripens the harvest.
- God releases His glory to those who diligently seek His face.

Till he comes and rains righteousness upon you

What a profound way for Hosea to end this prophetic admonition! If there were any doubts as to his mastery of agriculture, this certainly clears it up. Hosea knows that rainfall plays a most vital role in initiating and sustaining the growth of seeds, as well as in ripening the fruit for harvesting, in the natural.

In Hosea's day, there were two major seasons of rainfall-one at the start of seedtime, called the former rain, and another at the beginning of harvest time, called the latter rain. The purpose of the former rain was to moisten the ground for receiving the seed and to raise the underground water table to sustain growth after germination. It was the moisture from this former rain that made the trace elements or nutrients, in the earth, soluble enough for the plants to absorb them, via their roots, so that they could grow and mature, thereby. The latter rain came just at the point when the fruit began ripening in preparation for the harvest.

Hosea draws upon this knowledge of the mechanics of seedtime and harvest, in the natural, to emphasize the measure of the intensity with which those who wish to go beyond revival must seek the Lord. If we sow seeds of righteousness, then, we will need the trace elements of righteousness to promote growth and bring forth a bountiful harvest. Since this righteousness is not of human engineering, we must seek God, at all times, to pour it upon us, in such quantities and with such frequency that we will be caught in a continuous, ever-increasing downpour of virtual rain.

God loads into a torrential shower of righteousness every ingredient that we need to help take us from glory to glory. In it, we can find power for victorious living, anointing to work miracles, signs and wonders, revelation of His word, ability to live in unity with the brethren, strong determination to wage spiritual warfare, intense passion for the word, an insatiable hunger for being in the presence of the Lord and the power to bow before Him in genuine praise and worship. However, it is only those who are willing to go beyond the initial outbreak of anointing fire that will benefit from such a provision.

We may even go a little further and proclaim that the rain of righteousness also carries material benefits within its showers. Since righteousness is one of the pillars of the Kingdom of God, it stands to reason that anyone who seeks righteousness is also seeking the Kingdom of God. Jesus informs us, in Matthew 6:33, that if we set a premium on seeking the Kingdom of God and His righteousness, we will experience material increase.

Additionally, God promises, in Leviticus 26:3-12, that as long as we walk in obedience to His word, He will send us 'rain in due season'. Within this rain will come all the nutrients that will lead the 'land to yield her increase and the trees of the field to yield their fruit.' The fullness of this promise concerning the link between the rain of righteousness and material blessings, is found in Leviticus 26:9, AMP:

For I will be leaning towards you with favor and regard for you, rendering you fruitful, multiplying you, and establishing and ratifying my covenant with you.

In summing up this section, then, we need to put a mark of identification upon the underlying Kingdom principle built into Hosea 10:12. In this verse, Hosea basically celebrates the principle of continuity. Since God is everlasting and His Kingdom will never end, it stands to reason that, whenever He initiates a move within the Church, His desire is to transcend generations. A common addendum to His promises throughout the scriptures is 'The promise is to you and to your children.' There is no clearer expression of continuity than that.

It is no wonder, then, that God feels robbed, when an individual or ministry turns into a revival—a one cycle move of the Spirit—that which has the potential to move from a spark to a raging inferno and to become a lasting legacy unto Him. I prophesy to you that the next time God lights His fire in your life or in the ministry to which you belong, you will become the keeper of the flame. You will ensure that there is always an adequate flow of fuel to feed the fire, so that it never goes out. May the generations to come look back and call you blessed for passing on to them such a rich heritage, on which they can build.

In this season of the outpouring, continuity remains the principle upon which God desires to operate with His people. This is the reason that He has promised to send the rain of righteousness upon all who will seek His face with diligence. It is this rain, which will form the streams that will form into one deep, swift moving river. Like what happened with Ezekiel, it is this river into which the man with the measuring rod in his hand will take us beyond revival into the outpouring. We will move along a continuum of intense glory, from standing in ankle deep water near the shore to being pushed along by a swift moving flow of anointing. It is there that we can do nothing but go with the flow, because the waters of the Spirit have taken full control over us. The experience will be like being perpetually baptized in the Spirit.

Now that we know that God wants us to become more than thrill seekers, it is our prime responsibility to become even more passionate about seeking His face for the outpouring of that rain. His response will be to shower down upon us every element that we will need, making the experience last from one generation to another. Apostle Paul had insight of how this principle of continuity works. He writes, in Philippians 1:6, AMP:

I am convinced and sure of this one thing that He who began a good work in you is able to continue until the day of Jesus Christ.

*"After I have poured out my rains again,
I will pour out my Spirit upon all of you!"
(Joel 2:28, TLB).*

It's Time For
The Outpouring!

The term, OUTPOURING, literally refers to the unreserved, uninhibited release of fluid or liquid. It conjures up the picture of a container being turned upside down and its contents allowed flowing out until there is no more left. One may also see it in light of a faucet opened at full throttle with the water flowing continuously. However, the most vivid depiction of this, and most relevant to our discourse, is that of a heavy shower of rain falling upon the earth for long hours-a veritable downpour. Hence the reason Hosea uses the picture of a shower in his attempt to capture a sense of the dimensions of God's response to our deep hunger for His presence, person and power, as we explored in the previous chapter.

It is interesting to note that Hosea is not alone in the use of this particular imagery of rain to describe prophetically, God's response to the inward hunger of His people for more of Him. The prophetic writings of Joel and Peter's sermon on the day of Pentecost are strong cases in point.

Joel peers through his prophetic telescope and focuses on a time which he labels as the Day of the Lord (Joel 2:1). He records a description of what he sees in Joel 2, which seems to read like an amplified rendering of Hosea's admonition, in Hosea 10:12.

Bear in mind, though, to fully appreciate Joel's message here, one must understand the difference between the Now-Time and the Then-Time principles of end-time prophecy. It is the key to unlocking the full meaning of and connection between the terms 'Day of the Lord' in Joel 2:1 and 'a great people and strong' in Joel 2:2.

In the Then-Time dimension, the term, 'Day of the Lord', refers to the day when the Lord will physically return to earth to wage war against the armies of the Anti-Christ, as they gather against Israel at the Battle of Armageddon. In that case, the strong and mighty people, in focus, are most certainly the nation of Israel.

However, in the Now-Time dimension, 'Day of the Lord' has to be this present age or season of time in which we live, and which Peter labels as the Last Days in Acts 2:17. It means, then, that the great and mighty people to which Joel refers is the Church, over which Jesus has declared, "I will build my Church and the gates of Hell shall not prevail against it.' (Matthew 16:18' KJV).

If the above is true, then the world is in for a shocker because, according to Joel 2, it is about to find itself contending with a Church that refuses to be intimidated or marginalized anymore. As long as we are willing to take the steps to institute continuous ploughing up of the inner man, God intends to fix things so that we will no longer be a laughing stock to the world.

Here is a synopsis of the first segment of Joel's prophecy in Joel 2. Pay close attention to it, because adherence to and application of the truths, therein, will determine, to a large extent, the measure of the outpouring that is to come upon the Church.

Between verses 2 and 11 Joel gives a detailed pro file of the characteristics of this strong and mighty people (the Church), which God intends to raise up in this season. He celebrates their uniqueness in verse 2 by proclaiming that they are unlike any other that ever did or ever will walk the earth after them.

From verse 3 to 6, Joel proclaims that this end time people—the Church—will be so fearsome that they will instill terror and dread upon the rest of the world, as they subdue everything and everyone, before them, "Yea and nothing shall escape them... Before their face the people shall be much pained."

Verses 7 and 8 highlight the strong bond of unity and sense of purpose and destiny with which the Church will operate—"And they shall not break their ranks. Neither shall one thrust another; they shall walk everyone in his path."

Verse 9 suggests that the world may try, but will not succeed in keeping God's people out of the commanding heights of society, as in previous times. We will run through the cities looking for the legitimate points of entry into boardrooms of multi-national corporations and parliamentary chambers, et al. If we are denied entry through these points, then, we will take measures to force our way in through the windows like thieves or dismantle the roof like the men who brought their friend to Jesus. But to get in. we will get in. We are simply unstoppable

Verse 10 speaks of the Church wielding the dimensions of supernatural power that makes both the heavens and the earth recoil in fear.

Verse ii establishes what, in my opinion, is the most breathtaking feature of this end-time people: "And the Lord utters his voice before his army." God, Himself, intends to take the role of herald or outrider to announce the arrival, position, presence and passage of His people. He has a covenant with us to fulfill everything that He declares on our behalf—'For he is strong that execute his word.'

Having painted such a vivid picture of the strong and mighty people (the Church), which God is raising up in this season, Joel dedicates the rest of Joel 2 to giving an account of the strategy that God will use to accomplish this. He discerns that it is a four phased program, consisting of personal, corporate, economic and spiritual empowerment, in that order. It is absolutely important that we take heed to the order of things in this plan of God. As a result of not having done so, in the past, we have experienced untold frustration in our efforts to make headway, as we pursue our God-given dreams and visions.

The steps to personal empowerment are revealed between verses 12 and 14. These steps are a mirror image of Hosea's appeal in Hosea

10:12. With the same intensity, Joel admonishes, "Therefore also now, saith the Lord, turn ye even to me with all your heart, and with fasting...and rend your heart and not your garment." (Joel 2:12&13, KJV). Here, Joel is calling for the ploughing up of the inner man, using the excavating tools of deep soul searching, attitude adjustment and repentance. This is the gateway to God's grace, mercy, kindness and blessings coming upon the individual.

Then, from verse 15 to 19, Joel highlights phase two-corporate empowerment. In the Then-time dimension this is a call to national repentance for Israel, but in the Now-time dimension this call goes out to the Church, the Body of Christ in the earth. He advocates that there be special occasions, which he calls solemn assemblies, when the Church should gather for corporate prayer, fasting and sanctification. Note that at such times, the call is all-inclusive—the elders, the children, the babes in arms, and even the youths who have marriage on their minds must come.

At these solemn assemblies the priests and ministers must plead the causes of the people before God, imploring Him to forgive, cleanse and liberate them from the burdens imposed by heathen oppressors. The Lord's response will be to become passionate about redeeming the honor of his Church from the lips of the heathens— "Then will the Lord be jealous for his land (Church)...and I will make you no more a reproach among the heathen." (Joel 2:18&19).

The third phase of God's end-time strategy is the economic empowerment of His people, as recorded in verses 18 to 27. Here are the steps He will take to establish this.

In verse 19 He serves notice that He intends to take steps to eliminate every element that brought shame to His people, in the eyes of the heathen: "I will no longer make you a reproach among the heathen."

In verse 20, He vows to remove the forces that have oppressed His people for generations. One of the chief oppressors of God's people has tradition ally been the spirit of poverty. For years this spirit has been like serpents in our pockets that open their mouths to gobble up all our finances, and like monkeys on our backs, bringing ridicule, reproach and intimidation at the hands of the world's financial institutions. Well, God is covenanted with us to break that stranglehold for good. He will destroy the snakes and ladders syndrome under which we have been suffering financially. To do so, He will remove the snakes of debt and establish doors of opportunity for investments, so that His people can climb the ladder of prosperity out of poverty and lack.

In verses 20 and 21, He admonishes us that we should no longer be afraid because the desert places in our lives are about to spring forth with fruitfulness.

In verse 23, God wants us to bring out our tambourines and set our feet dancing, because whereas, in times past, He released blessings upon us in moderate measures, He now intends to pour them out like showers of rain. He will even compress time to hasten the flow of our blessings. In pursuit of this, He will send the former and latter rain upon us in the same month. In Old Testament times, these two seasons were at least six months apart—the former at seedtime and the latter at harvest time. It will be a sign of His willingness to hasten answers to our prayers.

Verse 24, (NIV), encourages us to get ready to own and manage businesses with large portfolios of properties and stocks: "And the threshing floors (factories and warehouses) shall be full of grain, and shall overflow with wine and oil (resources)." All of these are commodities that can be converted into cash in the market place.

Verse 25, (xiv), indicates that it is restoration time for those who have missed their jubilee years when their debts should have either been cancelled or paid in full. God will give back to us in great abundance all the resources that debt-creating circumstances have taken away from us: "I will repay you for the years that the locusts have eaten."

Verse 26 promises that the final proof of the economic empowerment of God's people will become evident where it matters most-at the dinner table in our homes: "Ye shall eat in plenty and be satisfied."

God's ultimate aim for the economic empowerment of His people is to give us a reason to praise Him. He knows that it is difficult to truly concentrate on praising and worshipping His name, when one cannot pay one's bills or feed one's family properly. Consequently, He says that when we become satisfied we shall 'praise the name of the Lord your God that hath dealt wondrously with you.' (Joel 2:26b). That will certainly help eliminate from our psyche the graphic picture of God as the operator of a convenience store on the corner. We will be so grateful for His bounty in our lives that we will be hard-pressed to present our grocery list, when we come into His presence. Instead, we will be delighting ourselves in worship and thanksgiving for His goodness.

The fourth phase of God's plan to create a strong and mighty people, in the end-time, involves spiritual empowerment. He gives clear details of each step between verses 28 and 32.

Unfortunately, the Church has traditionally taken this passage in isolation. Theologians have paid little or no attention to the sequence of events on God's schedule for empowerment, which we have just cited above. It is quite possible that they have been heavily influenced by Peter's declaration in Acts 2:17 in which he synopsizes the entire transformation process, recorded in Joel 2:1–27, into one expression—'In the Last Days? Yet, we must apply the Law of First Mention, in this case as well, to get a clear picture of God's true intentions for His Church.

Joel 2:28 begins with "And it shall come to pass afterward, that I shall pour out of my Spirit upon all flesh." Notice that Joel uses the expression "afterward' to pinpoint the time at which the outpouring will begin. The expression 'afterward' is an adverbial indicator of time, showing sequential progression. By it, God is saying, and has been saying all this time, that His intention is to bring His people into personal, corporate and economic empowerment before the full outpouring of His Spirit upon us. It is as though we have been putting the cart before the horse. We have been trying to do spiritual exploits without observing the following Kingdom principles, which are vital to the very survival of a move of God:

- Individual responsibility for an on-going personal relationship with God.

- The absolute necessity for unity of the Body of Christ. It is only with corporate effort that we can make lasting impact upon the world's system and truly enjoy the more abundant life that God has designated for us to live.
- The very anointing for speaking in tongues and healing the sick is also for generating finances. Wherever there is a lack of finances, it is difficult to pursue and fulfill vision.
- It is no wonder, then, why our efforts have only brought limited success.

Now that God has set in motion the first three phases of His strategy for empowering the Church, He is ready to activate the fourth, which is spiritual empowerment. He now feels free to truly flood the Church with the anointing to see visions, dream dreams and to work signs, wonders and miracles. God knows that we will not fail this time around, because individuals and entire congregations will see it as their responsibility before God to do whatever is necessary to maintain the fire. Moreover, empowered by a new mindset, concerning money and wealth, and generating a more powerful cash flow, the Church will step into the marketplace to become a worthy partner in managing the commanding heights of the economy.

Joel's take on what is about to unfold is that this raging torrent of the anointing will permeate every stratum of the Church, in particular, and of society in general, engineering nothing less than a spiritual revolution. Herein lies the essence of the revolution. In the season when this outpouring occurs, God has promised that 'I shall pour out of my spirit upon all flesh.'

Pay careful attention to the fact that it is not only sons (males) who shall prophesy under the power of the anointing, but also daughters (females). Neither in Joel's day nor in our day does the religious hierarchy readily accept the latter. Notwithstanding, change is here. Additionally, old men who are traditionally put on the shelf of retirement will suddenly find new spiritual energy. They will go in hot pursuit of dreams that they have long abandoned as impossible.

Furthermore, young men will no longer drift about aimlessly but will become visionaries in search of their destiny and purpose.

It is for this reason that God intends to empower His people economically, as a precursor to the full flow of the outpouring of the Spirit. He knows that for the old men to truly make their dreams come true, for the young men to fulfill their visions and for the daughters to realize their prophetic potential, they will need financial and material resources in great volume.

So many individuals and ministries, today, cannot accomplish their goals because they are strapped for both cash and adequate facilities. There is no doubt that the anointing is heavy upon many of them, as evidenced by the quality of worship, praise and intercession, which they generate when they assemble.

However, because of ignorance, many have paid little regard to creating a sound financial base. Consequently, as their visions enlarge, they experience grave difficulties and frustrations in making them a reality. It is my firm belief that we need to take another look at this prophetic word from Joel and ask God to align us to His sequence of doing things. As long as we come into alignment and stay aligned to God's way of doing things, the flames of fire will never go out, once they are lit among us. The anointing that floods the atmosphere, as the Spirit of God is being outpoured will be the source of perpetual supply from which we will get the fuel to feed the fire.

Here is a prophetic synopsis of what we have just discussed above:

> The outpouring has begun. It is bringing personal and corporate empowerment to the Church, economic prosperity to God's people and releasing wave after wave of the anointing to do signs, wonders and miracles. Get your vessels ready and position yourselves where the rain is falling, so that you may be filled to the overflowing. In this season, positioning is everything. Where you are mentally, psycho logically, financially, spiritually and physically, in this season of the outpouring, will determine not only what you get out of it, but also, what

you become, because of it. Stay in alignment to God's purpose and the fire will never go out.

In delivering his sermon on the Day of Pentecost, Apostle Peter quotes directly from the writings of Joel, as he attempts to put in perspective the strange phenomenon occurring in the Upper Room. He declares:

> *This is that which was spoken by the prophet Joel, And it shall come to pass in the last days, saith God, I will pour out of my spirit upon all flesh: and your sons and daughters shall prophesy, and your young men shall see visions, and your old men shall dream dreams: and on my servants and on my hand maidens I will pour out of my spirit in those days and they shall prophesy.' (Acts 2:16–18).*

By this declaration, Peter cites the Day of Pentecost as the beginning of the prophetic season known as the Last Days, but which Joel calls the Day of the Lord. If this was two thousand years ago, then, it means that today we are at the very end of that season.

If we consider that when substances are being poured out the flow increases both in volume and intensity over time, then, in this season we are about to be swamped by waves and waves of irrefutable evidence of the presence of the Holy Spirit in our lives and ministries. It means that what Joel prophesied and what occurred both on and subsequent to the Day of Pentecost will happen again, in our time. However, this time around it will be on a wider front and with greater frequency and intensity. The visible evidence of tongues of fire, the prophetic tongues, the utterance of revelation from the lips of the most unlikely and the mass intake of souls will be common occurrences throughout the earth, as God's people seek His face in earnest.

Already there are documented reports of such developments and even stranger phenomena occurring. Here is a short list of some of these reports from around the globe.

Note also, though, that, even as I am editing this work in 2007, many of these moves of God that were raging infernos in 1999–2000, the time frame of most of the copies of Charisma Magazine from which the information comes, have petered out into nothingness or have become smoldering embers, at best. When examined in light of what was discussed in Chapter Two—'WHY DO MOVES OF GOD DIE'—we will see that many of them came into their demise because the leaders and commentators perceived of them as merely 'revivals'. As such, they failed to develop a mindset for the outpouring and the principle of continuity upon which it operates. Consequently, the fire was starved for fuel, as the lines became clogged with chunks of the debris described in Chapter Two. What is very frightening is the fact that, from the little research that I have done, once a fire goes out in a particular place it seems as though God takes a long time to rekindle it, if at all. Just think about how long it took for the door to Canaan to re-open to Israel and the many that died in the forty year interim and that should be incentive enough to drive us to maintain the glory fire that we obtain.

N.B. All information appearing in this segment has been sourced from issues of Charisma Magazine, produced by Strang Communications Company of Lake Mary, Florida and reproduced either through direct quotes or edited abridgements.

- The Toronto Blessing Revival, which began in January 1994 at the Toronto Airport Christian Fellowship in Canada, shows 110 signs of waning after six years. On any given night of the six nights per week services one can find visitor's from Germany, Wales, Japan and other far flung places around the globe, joining with native Canadians in hilarious praise and worship unto the Lord.
- Brownsville Assembly of God in Pensacola, Florida. An evangelist, Steve Hill, who came to this assembly to minister at the morning service on Father's Day, 1995, over five years ago is still there holding services five days per week together with the Pastor and other ministers. Hundreds of thousands

of people from around the world have visited this outpouring since the outbreak. Pastors among them have gone back to their churches and have reported that the same type of worship and manifestations of Holy Spirit are happening in their own ministries.

- God invades a Nowhere' Place: The youth services on Wednesday nights at the Marysville First Assembly, in Seattle, Washington USA, are drawing a crowd so big it spills into the aisles, foyer and adjoining fellowship hall. As teens surge forward, in response to altar calls, it is not uncommon to see many fall to their knees in demonstration of repentance and total surrender to God. Others shake and collapse to the floor as they receive anointed prayer from altar workers. In a city that is as un churched as they come in the USA, this certainly is a phenomenon. Seattle, city that boasts of being headquartered city for Microsoft and other multi-national conglomerates, has been experiencing a serious drug and crime problem among its youths for years. Says Youth Pastor Benny Perez, "God is going to use youths to catapult America (and indeed the world) back into revival and to its knees."
- The Holy Spirit visits Ireland. In a land known for spiritual darkness and sectarian violence for the better part of a century, God is now pouring out His love and power upon those who seek Him. Amid the sounds of bombs and bullets, another sound is becoming increasingly louder. It is the sound of prayer warriors pleading the cause of Ireland before God. Many of these intercessors are coming from foreign lands with a divine mandate to ignite the fire of intercessory prayer within the spirits of the Irish Christians who themselves have been seeking the face of the Father for spiritual breakthrough. In over two hundred churches across the nation, doors are opened at six o'clock every morning for intercessory prayer. Hundreds of people, including children dressed for school, stream through these open doors, head straight for the altar, and fall on their faces before God. The

power of the Holy Spirit is falling upon them, with evidence of speaking in tongues, signs, wonders and miracles. Can this be the reason that the IRA, the Protestants and the British Government are now earnestly conducting peace talks after years of sectarian violence?

- Fresh Fire From Down Under: After years of noticeable decline in church attendance in Australia, God burst on the scene with revival fire in 1994. Australia has been set ablaze and to date there seems to be no sign of the fire waning.
- Argentine Revival Fire has been ablaze for the last fifteen years and just seems to be getting hotter. Its outbreak came on the heels of years of fervent prayer whichtook the form of prayer walks, all night vigils in churches and sports arenas and sessions of spiritual warfare in trouble spots where witchcraft and the occult held people in bondage. It is reported that over these fifteen years approximately 4 million people have become born-again Christians in a traditionally Roman Catholic nation. One of the leaders of the movement, Rev. Freidzon, in counseling a group of ministers in the USA concerning the sustenance of revival fire gave the same advice, in principle, as what the Lord has revealed in this prophecy. He advised, "If a sweeping revival is to be sustained, it must be built on four priorities: holiness, worship, evangelism and the teaching of the Word of God."
- Revival in China appears unstoppable despite persecution. In one province, a revival that began six years ago has already claimed over 200,000 souls for Christ. The revival is so widespread that Pastors work for long hours every day just baptizing converts. Many of the evangelists today are youths who were part of the Tiananmen Square demonstrations of 1989. Although the communist regime continues to jail and torture many pastors and believers, the fierce oppression only results in more conversions as these Christians continue to spread the gospel behind bars. Two sisters encapsulated the general fervor of the Church in China in their reply to a question concerning the possibility of incarceration

for attending church, "We would welcome it as another opportunity to share with the police and other prisoners the love of Jesus."

- When God came to England: Churches in England have been engulfed in a flood of revival fervor since 1994. Emerging like an army from the mists of spiritual renewal, the church in England is sounding a new battle cry, 'It's time for revival. A key figure in the movement is Pastor Sandy Millar, vicar of Holy Trinity Brompton, where this fresh wave of the Holy Spirit broke out in the summer of 1994. Evangelist Steve Hill, who is accredited with starting the Brownsville Revival in 1995 reports that it was after Millar had prayed for him on a visit to Holy Trinity in 1994 that the Holy Spirit came upon him in such a mighty life changing way. Millar sums up the phenomenon like this, "We believe God is refreshing his Church."

- Latin America's Sweeping Revival: Researchers say that 400 people are converted to Christianity every hour in South and Central America. During the last fifteen years the number of Latin American full gospel Christians has increased from 18.6 million to over 70 million. The revival is transforming the religious landscape. A steady stream of converts is flowing into the Pentecostal churches from both the Roman Catholic and protestant denominations. Pentecostals represent over 66% of non-Catholic Christians. In Peru, a new church is planted every eight hours. In Rio de Janeiro, Brazil, at least one new congregation is born every day.

- Cuban Churches thrive amid continued harassment: A Florida based evangelist, Barry Owensbey, who has made over twenty-two trips to Cuba since 1990 says churches in the communist island are growing at a phenomenal rate despite continued harassment from Fidel Castro's government. Owensbey reports that there is unusual openness to the gospel on the island, and the churches are most definitely in a state of revival.

- Unusual Manifestations: Recently (late 1990's), many churches in the USA have reported that when the glory of God comes down unusual manifestations occur; including the appearance of gold dust and dental healings involving gold fillings. However, for churches in South America this is not new. In Argentina it has been occurring since in the early 1990's and it is so widespread that only people who have had at least three gold fillings are allowed to testify in public.

There is so much more documented evidence of the on-going outpouring of the Spirit upon the earth that lack of space greatly restricts us from including all of it in a work of this nature. I recommend that you get hold of copies of the 'Charisma' magazine from as far back as 1994 to present and see for yourself. I also recommend that you go to the World Wide Web and just type in 'Revival' on Google Search and it will amaze you to see the measure of His Spirit that God is pouring out upon all flesh.

The Gamaliel Principle

You may be reading this right now and are suddenly realizing that occurrences of a similar nature have been happening to you, each time you come into God's presence or each time your congregation assembles for worship. For example:

- Worship songs, which have never been sung in the earth before, come forth spontaneously, on a frequent basis.
- You go before God with a prayer list, only to realize that, at the end of the session, you have spent more time worshipping and seeking His face than asking Him for things.
- Without any altar call being made, people, many of them new converts, are lying prostrate at the altar of the church, during the worship session or while the minister is delivering his message.

- Personal and corporate prophecies are being proclaimed within the congregation, with great regularity and pinpoint accuracy, bringing transformation to individuals and to the congregation, in general.
- People are seeing life changing dreams and visions.
- Miracles, healings, deliverances, debt cancellations, unusual releases of finances and mush rooming of new business establishments are occurring in increasing volume.
- Pastor stands to deliver a prepared sermon, but God breaks through with such a powerful river of revelation that he has no choice but to prophesy.
- Without any organized evangelism program, God is adding people to the church daily in great numbers.
- People are reporting of having encounters with angels.

Now you know for sure that you are not going mad. On the contrary, you are right on the cutting edge of what God is doing among His people, at this time. Like Elijah, you now realize that you are a part of a larger company of people who are accessing God at this whole new level. What you need to do is document and date those experiences for future reference. You will have the evidence to help someone else make sense out of what is happening in his or her life.

On the other hand, such manifestations of the Spirit may not have yet begun to occur in your neck of the woods. There is no need to get frustrated Instead, you should get both excited and expectant. Be ever mindful that the promise is for Holy Spirit to fall upon all flesh. I am sure you qualify. Look at the steps to soul preparation listed in an earlier segment and apply them to your life. At the same time, make a covenant to encourage others to do the same. I prophesy to you that God will respond to your hunger by flooding your life and the ministry with which you are covenanted with an outpouring of Holy Spirit that you will not be able to contain.

However, you may belong to that category of people who are very skeptical and critical about the moves of God. May I admonish you that you are treading on dangerous grounds, if you choose to make premature pronouncements of condemnation and criticisms! Over the years that I have been in the Church, I have seen people stand on the sidelines and level criticisms at others who dared to flow with the Spirit. Some have even tried to jump into the stream in a vain attempt to stop the river from flowing. Such indiscretions have always been to their chagrin and sometimes demise. I solemnly warn you that it is impossible to stop this move of God.

Just like with Isaac, God has dug His final well in His Church and is not going to stand by and let anyone fill it up this time. This well of the anointing is bursting forth in an ever-increasing flow. It is flowing from under the very throne of God to form a raging river that is moving everything before it. No man, except maybe Joshua, has ever yet been able to stand in the midst of a flooded river in the natural and command the waters to stop flowing, and that was under divine direction. Since God will not give anyone the authority to stop the flow of His anointing, you should know that you are courting swift, decisive, divine judgment, if you attempt to do so.

Do not make the mistake of condemning what you do not understand to hell's fire and brimstone. Rather, put it on the back burner on a low fire and wait for the Lord to show you what is happening. If time proves that it was not really a move of God, in the first place, you would not have lost anything. However, as long as it is of God, the truth will prevail. Now, where would that place you if you had been part of the chorus of voices that sought to discredit it? You may have to answer to God, not only for yourself, but also for the many people that you may have caused to miss their season of spiritual breakthrough, by way of you having voiced your skepticism.

You may be better served, if you adopt the attitude of Gamaliel, a member of the Sanhedrin Council, when he stood to make his pronouncement during the interrogation of Peter and the other apostles in Acts 5. He solemnly warned the other members of the council:

> *Refrain from these men, and let them alone: for if this counsel or work be of men, it will come to naught: But if it be of God, you cannot overthrow it: lest haply ye may be found even to fight against God. (Acts 5:39).*

Liquid Power

At the beginning of the previous chapter, we defined the term outpouring as the unreserved, uninhibited release of liquids or fluids. Based on this definition and on the behavior of rain, in the natural, we have been able to categorize Hosea's 'rain of righteousness', in Hosea 10:12, as an allusion to the outpouring of the anointing of the Holy Spirit upon the Church and upon individuals, as well.

When a real heavy shower of rain falls, in the natural, commentators are wont to describe the phenomenon as the clouds bursting and pouring out their contents upon the earth like an overturned barrel. In essence, this is the picture that Joel tries to paint in Joel 2:28—the cloud of God's glory bursting forth and He showering His anointing upon us, in the earth. However, when we search through scripture, we discover that rain (water) is only one of the many liquid or fluid substances that writers use in their attempt to capture the true nature, scope, function and behavior of the Holy Spirit, when he flows among us.

Let us now revisit this line of discussion and see what additional truths we may glean that will facilitate adequate preparation to receive and appropriate the outpouring of the Holy Spirit, in this season. Our line of approach will be to identify these liquids and fluids. In the process, we will highlight a few scriptures in which they are used in metaphors, allusions and illustrations, pertaining to the Holy Spirit. Then, we will enter into a more in-depth discussion on the significance of wine in scripture and how an appreciation of its physical properties, in a prophetic dimension, can help to take us beyond revival where we will become caught up in the raging currents of the outpouring

Water

In his discussions with the woman at the well, Jesus showed her that she could go beyond just having a religious experience. Instead, she could live in the realm of the perpetual outpouring of the Holy Spirit. Alluding to the well of natural water from which she was waiting to draw, he said, "But whoever shall take a drink of the water that I shall give him shall never, no never, be thirsty anymore. But the water that I shall give him shall become a spring of water welling up (flowing, bubbling) continually within him unto (into, for) eternal life." (John 4:14, AMP).

Milk

Peter's admonition to the Church, in 1 Peter 2:1&2, is very instructive for proper preparation for and effective maintenance of the anointing fire. Peter understands that, among nutritionists, milk is regarded as the complete food. Therefore, he concluded that anyone who develops a hunger for God's word, in much the same manner as a child desires its mother's milk, will experience a level of nutrition that will sustain consistent growth. Here is what Peter had to say: "Wherefore laying aside all malice, and all guile, and hypocrisies, and envies, and all evil speaking, as new born babes, desire the sincere milk of the word, (pure spiritual milk) that ye may grow thereby." This is the essence of living in the dimension called the outpouring.

Milk is also a symbol of the prosperity that comes with the outpouring. God promised Israel that after He had delivered them from Egyptian slavery He would take them to Canaan, 'a land flowing with milk and honey.' (Exodus 3:8). In the analogy, based on its liquid or fast flowing nature, milk represents a cash flow that takes complete care of current expenses.

Honey

For the honey bee, honey is not only the commodity that they produce; it is also the food that nourishes and sustains them. Except for the obvious absence of the whiteness that milk carries, honey is just as complete a food for the bee as milk is for animals. When used in scripture, therefore, honey is a symbol of the richness of the divine revelation that comes with the outpouring of the Spirit. In recounting the manner in which he received fresh revelation from God,

> *Ezekiel stated, "And he said to me, Son of man eat this scroll that I give you and fill your stomach with it. Then I ate it and it was sweet as honey in my mouth." (Ezekiel 3:3, AMP).*

Additionally, as indicated above, honey is also part of the metaphor that God used to describe the level of prosperity that Israel would enjoy in Canaan. By deduction, then, honey is also an analogy of the prosperity that comes with every new move of God. In such a case, since honey is a fluid, which means that it oozes instead of flows, it represents the returns from medium and long term investments. Although they may be long in coming, they do make life sweet, when they arrive.

Oil

Oil was the fuel that kept the lamps burning continually, in both the tabernacle and the temple, two places in which God traditionally met with Israel (Exodus 27:20). Since both the Church and the individual are now the dwelling places of God, in the earth, it stands to reason that the Lord expects to see a fire burning continually within us also. The only way that this can be accomplished is for us to have the Holy Spirit consistently flowing within us as an active oil well, fuelling the anointing fire (Psalms 23:5).

Oil was also the main ingredient in the mixture with which Moses anointed Aaron as high priest and his sons as priests. Having instructed Moses to dress Aaron in the robes of the High Priest, in Exodus 29:6, God now tells him, in Exodus 29:7, NIV, to 'take the anointing oil and anoint him (Aaron) by pouring it on his head.' This is exactly what God wants to do with all those of us who belong to the royal priesthood when He pours out His Spirit upon His people, in this season of the outpouring.

Additionally, oil also symbolizes the euphoria that comes upon a people who are caught up in a life changing move of God in which the Holy Spirit is being allowed freedom of expression. Isaiah prophesies that for all those who are mourning in Zion (the Church), God will give the oil of joy and gladness instead of mourning and sorrow. (Isaiah 61:3).

Oil is a by-product, a fuel and a lubricant all at the same time, as far as the all-important principle of unity is concerned. It was in an atmosphere of unity that the first major outbreak of anointing fire erupted in the Upper Room (Acts 2). As long as the Church remained in one accord, the oil of unity kept the fire burning until the entire then-known world was set on fire. This was, undoubtedly, a manifestation of what David wrote in Psalms 133 in celebration of the absolutely vital role that the oil of unity plays as a factor in the equation that produces and sustains the outpouring. When the oil of unity flows, it lubricates the relationship between the leader of the move of God (Aaron), secondary leadership (Aaron's beard) and the rest of the congregation (the skirts of Aaron's garments). Here is what David had to say in Psalms 133:1&2, AMP: "BEHOLD, HOW good and how pleasant it is for brethren to dwell together in unity! 2 It is like the precious ointment poured on the head, that ran down on the beard, even the beard of Aaron (the first high priest), that came down upon the collar and skirts of his garments (consecrating the whole body)." In short, the oil of unity promotes continuity.

Finally, oil is a metaphor for the Holy Spirit in his role as yoke destroyer and burden remover. In light of what we discussed in an earlier chapter, this is an essential truth for the Church to receive, especially in this season of the outpouring. We learnt that as soon as the anointing fire breaks out, the devil takes it as his duty to impose upon it weights and impediments to snuff it out or at least to retard its progress. However, as long as the Holy Spirit is allowed to have full control, he exercises his authority over proceedings as a manifestation of Isaiah 10:27, NKJV: "It shall come to pass in that day That his burden will be taken away from your shoulder, And his yoke from your neck, And the yoke will be destroyed because of the anointing oil." The NIV suggests that the oil (The Holy Spirit) will make our necks so far that yokes and burdens will not be able to go around them anymore. That sounds like continuous success against all odds to me. So let the oil flow.

Blood

Leviticus 17:11 teaches that the real life of the body is in the blood that runs through its circulatory system. If that blood drains out without a simultaneous infusion, then, that body is sure to die. The quality of life that the body enjoys is directly related to the quality and quantity of blood that circulates through it. Hence the reason that eating the right foods is so important.

It is the nutrients provided by food that stimulate the marrow within the bones to create the plate lets, which help to enrich the quality of the blood in our bodies. In turn, the blood is able to carry out its special function of transporting throughout the body, building blocks of life such as oxygen, vitamins, minerals and other nutrients to promote vitality and wellbeing. At the same time, it cleanses the body by removing death dealing particles like car bon dioxide.

It stands to reason, then, that if the Church is the Body of Christ and Holy Spirit represents the life of Christ in the Church, it behooves us all to allow the Holy Spirit to flow unhindered through the Church. He is the one who carries the word of God into our inner man to stimulate growth and maturity. At the same time, he uses the word and the blood of Jesus to cleanse the souls of all who desire to live pure in the sight of God. It is no wonder, then, that there is so great an emphasis on repentance and spiritual renewal whenever there is an outpouring of Holy Spirit upon a people.

It follows naturally, then, that the greater the freedom, which we allow the Holy Spirit, it is the greater vitality of the Zoë life that we will experience in the Church in ordinary times and, certainly, when there is a definitive outpouring of Holy Spirit. Why not make way for Holy Spirit to move in your life!

Balm/Ointment

Jeremiah 8:22, AMP, ask the question "Is there no balm in Gilead? Is there no physician there? Why then is not the health of the daughter of my people restored? (Because Zion no longer had the presence of the Great Physician.)"

Whenever there is a sudden outbreak of anointing fire in a church, answers to this question manifest in the proliferation of testimonies about spectacular healings and deliverances. These healings are not only physical, but also emotional and spiritual. The debilitating effects of emotional wounds, verbal abuse, low self-esteem, unforgiveness and broken homes, to name just a few, are cancelled. The ex victims now walk the earth with a new assurance and confidence that they could be of some value to both God and mankind.

Yes, when the outpouring begins to flow, Holy Spirit shows up as a balm and ointment to soothe our hurts and heal our diseases. This is the promise God makes to us in Jeremiah 30:17 and Isaiah 61:1:

> *Jeremiah 30:17, NLT: I will give you back your health and heal your wounds, says the Lord.*

Isaiah 61:1, NKJV:...He has sent Me to heal the brokenhearted, To proclaim liberty to the captives, And the opening of the prison to those who are bound;...

Virtue

When the woman with the issue of blood had come to the end of both herself and her resources, she made a decision in the face of great odds to come within touching distance of Jesus. Upon touching the hem of Jesus' garment, she found a new lease on life, in at least two dimensions. She received physical healing as evidenced by the instantaneous stanching of the flow of blood. At the same time, she also experienced the transfusion of the very life of Christ into her inner being. Jesus knew exactly when the transfusion took place because he commented to his disciples that he felt virtue flow out of him.

If one understands the power of the Zoë life, it will not be difficult to see this woman leaving the presence of Jesus completely transformed. At one moment she projects the perfect picture of a victim of Satan, that old thief. In the very next instance, she is walking in the more abundant life that Jesus gives.

This is exactly the experience that comes to any individual or ministry that makes a decision to touch the heart of God with worship, prayer, praise and obedience. God pours out His spirit, as virtue or the Zoë life upon them. In an instant, that individual begins to walk the earth, as though he is more than a conqueror. He develops a new sense of destiny and impacts others for God. That ministry, in its turn, begins to make a mark for God, on the community, national and global levels. It moves from being a nonentity, hidden in a corner to being the place to which everyone wants to come and with which everyone wants to identify. When virtue flows, the fire never goes out.

Wine

At its very basic level, wine is actually the juice extracted from the grape. Mankind has been known to use it at different stages, ranging from the very moment that it comes from the winepress to a point in time, many years later, after it has gone through a process of fermentation and distillation.

To fully appreciate the significance of wine as a symbol of the anointing, during this time of the out pouring, one has to focus on its definition on the figurative plane. At this level, the grape becomes merely a container that collects and stores the wine that, in reality, comes from the vine that bears the grape. Hence, in John 15, Jesus identifies himself as the 'true vine'. He also classifies the Father as the husbandman' and us as 'branches'. He admonishes us to stay connected to him, so that we can produce the grape to receive and store the wine.

By identifying himself as the 'true vine', Jesus alerts us to the fact that there is a false vine lurking in the wings, wishing to deceive us into attaching ourselves to him instead. Without actually saying it, therefore, Jesus shouts loudly into our ears, "Be not deceived! Get to know the difference! It is what will determine how closely you come to fulfilling your divine destiny."

Additionally, Jesus also brings into focus the spiritual union between himself and the Church. He does this by standing on the premise that in the natural the quality of life that the branch enjoys is directly related to its ability to stay connected to the vine. It is that connection that allows the branch to receive the life-giving sap that flows into it from the vine, providing nutrients for growth and fruit bearing. A clear grasp of this metaphor is especially essential, as we strive to go beyond the traditional understanding of revival, in our quest to live in the outpouring.

In an earlier segment, we established two vital principles, crucial to our journey to and survival in that state called 'The Outpouring'. We concluded that "Whatever we obtain, we must maintain to retain'. In applying that law to the nature of a fire, we discovered that if we obtain fire and we wish to retain or make full use of the flame, then we must maintain the flow of fuel that ignited the spark in the first place.

Then, we applied these laws to the phenomenon known as 'revival fire and finally deciphered why revivals generally have such a short life span. The fundamental problem is the failure of the average individual or assembly to continue flowing in the same vein of prayer, fasting, worship, repentance and uncompromising obedience, which initiated the move of God.

Now that this revelation has unfolded much more clearly, I see another even more debilitating principle within the equation. It seems as though immediately as the anointing fire breaks out an overriding spirit called ignorance, swings into operation. What is the essence of this ignorance? It is ignorance of what really constitutes (1) the life of the Church and (2) the life of any move of God in the Church.

It is ignorance that makes one believe that it is my prayer and fasting or our new attitude to worship that initiates and sustains the move of God. Nothing could be further from the truth! The truth is that the Church is the Body of Christ and is alive only as long as the life of Christ flows through it. Add to this the analogy of Christ as the true vine', God as the 'husbandman' and we as the 'branches' and we must agree that any outbreak of anointing fire, in the Church, is solely a sovereign move of God, in response to our obedience to His will.

Since this is so, one must agree that the lifespan of that anointing fire will always be directly proportion ate to the volume of the Zoë life allowed to flow into an individual or ministry. Also, considering the fact that the Zoë life or life of Christ is obtainable only by way of one's ongoing relationship with Christ, the true vine, it is incumbent upon all to stay connected to him. Satan knows the effect that such a connection creates, so his plan will always be to deceive us into severing it or, at least, weaken it, so that the flow of sap/virtue may be reduced to a trickle.

Consequently, whenever there is a move of God, there is a grave need for even greater vigilance on the part of all concerned. In much the same way that callous material can develop at the point where the branch joins the vine, thus stanching the flow of life giving sap, so too can disobedience, ignorance and pride create insensitivity to the Lord's desires, effectively choking out the flow of the Zoë life. The end result, in the natural, is always death to the branch. Similarly, in the Spirit, a severing or weakening of the God/man union eventually brings death to the move of God.

This information may surprise some and excite many, but God becomes more vigilant in His handling of an individual or ministry, which is caught up in one of His sovereign moves. He regards the release of His anointing upon a people as His investment into their lives. He expects His investment to yield results that would redound to the benefit of His Kingdom. He looks for results in the Christ-like manner in which people conduct themselves and interact with one another. He also measures results by the degree of passion with which His people go after the Kingdom life. In short, God comes among His people, in the time of the outpouring, in search of the fruit of the Spirit, as recorded in Galatians 5:22, because outpouring time is fruit bearing time.

Here is where the Father's role, as the husband man, really kicks in. Jesus warns that during such times, the Father pays regular visits to the vineyard (the Church) to assess the condition of the branches. Each visit has a two-fold purpose and according to what He finds, He takes appropriate action. John 15:2, AMP, gives a very precise account of what transpires during a typical visit by the Father to the Church:

> Any branch (believer) in me that does not bear fruit-that stops bearing-He cuts away (trims off, takes away). And He cleanses and repeatedly prunes every branch that continues to bear fruit, to make it bear more and richer and more excellent fruit.

By way of application to the way in which God operates in His Church in such times, this verse carries a double-edged paradox. On the one hand, a ministry that is enveloped in a sovereign move of God may experience a great influx of new believers, while at the same time see a falling away of its established membership who refuse to flow with the new season. On the other hand, although that ministry may seem to be operating at a higher level of impact than others around it, it may yet find its worship services being regularly punctuated with prophetic declarations such as, 'Repent!' 'Return unto your first love!' 'Amend your ways and your doings! In essence, God is taking steps to ensure the expansion and longevity of the anointing fire in that place.

There is also this ultra-sensitivity that develops within members of the assembly, concerning the presence of God. Like David in Psalms 27:4, a discernable fire of desire burns within each heart for being in the house of God. It is as though spiritual meteorologists show up in every service to take readings on the temperature (intensity of passion for God), rainfall (rate and volume of the outpouring) and barometric (flow of Holy Spirit as a wind) conditions within the atmosphere of the assembly. Whenever these readings are not at the optimum level, the Holy Ghost always sets the trumpet to someone's mouth to sound an alarm for a return to basics.

For the Father, in His role as husbandman, the sequence of events, described above, are simply His way of conducting routine maintenance of His vineyard. Although to the uninitiated observer some of His measures may seem harsh and unorthodox, His aim is purely to improve the viability of the vineyard (the Church), increase its impact upon the world and ensure the profitability of His investment. In reality, God is adhering, without any apology, to his own Kingdom law, "From everyone who has been given much, much shall be required." (Luke 12:48, NAS).

In the process, the Father teaches us four additional principles, vital for experiencing a perpetual outpouring of the Holy Spirit:

- Where we are with God hinges not on where others are with Him but on where He has ordained for us to be.
- My righteousness is not determined by the righteousness of others, but by my obedience to the word of God.
- Where I am determines what I receive.

- Position yourself where God wants you to be and He will give you access to all that you need to have.

Here is a short list of very noteworthy truths, which have emerged, thus far, from our exploration of wine as a symbol of the outpouring. Not the least of these is the truth that sap, wine, anointing and Zoë life are one and the same.

- Just like blood in animals, sap is the solution that carries life-giving nutrients throughout the plant. Similarly, the anointing is the medium that brings the fullness of the Zoë life of God to the Body of Christ.
- When fruit-bearing time comes along, it is the same sap that provides the plant with the raw material to form the grape, which becomes the container for storing the juice and the seeds. In much the same way, when the time of outpouring comes, it is the anointing that drives us to prepare the inner man to receive an extra-ordinary release of the Zoë life. The anointing also provides us with the power to manifest the gifts and fruit of the Spirit.
- In the vine, the juice is the wine and the grape acts as the first container. In the Spirit, this extra ordinary release of Zoë life is called the new wine and our inner man is the receptacle.

Preparing For the New Wine

Let us look at another body of truths that we can glean from the vine as it pertains to our response to the divine mandate upon us for this season.

- The grape displays the quality and character of the vine upon which it hangs. We too must display the character and person of Christ, our true vine.
- The skin of the grape must be stretchable to accommodate the wine with which it is being filled. The child of God who

desires to be filled with the new wine must become pliable and yielded in the hands of God.

- The grape must remain on the vine until maturity or else its wine will not be fit for use. For the new wine to be of any value to us both in life and in ministry, we must enter this season of the outpouring, for the long haul and not for some overnight thrill.
- The grape must have staying power, even in the face of the fiercest of extremes in the weather such as storms, rain and scorching sunshine. In this time of the outpouring, we must be aware of the aim of the enemy to separate us from our source, rendering us totally ineffective. Therefore, the child of God who desires to make an impact, at this time, must make the same declaration that Paul made in Romans 8:38&39: "For I am persuaded that neither death, nor life, nor angels, nor principalities, nor powers, nor things present, nor things to come, nor height, nor depth, nor any other creature, shall be able to separate us from the love of God, which is in Christ Jesus our Lord."
- Grapes bear in bunches. Survival in the bunch rests upon two basic principles—unity and tolerance. Each grape must make way for the others to draw sap from the vine, even though it may mean being squeezed out of shape by others that may sit upon it in their efforts to do so. Those that do not comply usually shrivel up and die. In this season of the outpouring, there is a renewed clarion call for the Psalms 133 principle of unity to become active in the Body of Christ. We must develop the cluster mentality, especially since it is well known that it is in such times that the enemy would like to divide and rule. Even though we may have personality clashes, at times, it is incumbent upon us to forgive and give preference to one another. Such an attitude is what helps to shape the character of Christ in us. Isaiah 65:8 clearly teaches, "The new wine is found in the cluster."

What is this New Wine?

Wine makers place the label, New Wine, on wines at opposite ends of the processing continuum. On the one hand, this label is placed on the first wine-that juice which the grape releases voluntarily, when it bursts under the sheer pressure of being clustered with others, in the trough of the winepress. Wine makers regard this as the best, clearest, tastiest, most valuable and most precious of all. They cherish it as the one most suited for aging into special, high quality, high priced wines.

In this season of the outpouring, the accent will be on worship that comes spontaneously and joy fully from the heart, as distinct from the one that some worship leader has to squeeze out of us. It is that worship, for which the Lord has highest respect and in which He delights most greatly. This is what Jesus meant when he told the woman at the well, 'But the hour cometh, and now is, when the true worshippers will worship the Father in spirit and in truth, for the Father seeketh such to worship hin1." John 4:23). The Father's response to this quality of worship is always the release of an outpouring of His Spirit, the new wine 'that makes glad the heart', upon his people, so that their own bellies or spirits overflow with living water.

On the other end of the production continuum, new wine refers to wine that has just been distilled and bottled after having been left to ferment in casks for a long period. It may have been set to age from 'first wine' or from juice extracted by trampling/ crushing the grapes in the trough of the winepress.

Wine from the winepress

After removing the first or new wine, trained workers at the winery now set about extracting the rest of the juice from the grapes. In Bible times, they did so by tran1pling upon the grapes in the trough of the winepress, crushing the flesh to release the juice.

Is this not somewhat like what God does with us: Even when we may be doing well in our overall obedience to Him, He knows that there is more worship, more praise, more ministry and more intercession within us, hidden behind the veil of our flesh. Consequently, He lays us upon His winepress (altar) and arranges for circumstances to come our way in which specially gifted people seem to take a delight in trampling all over us. We bawl and howl, when we feel the pain. We rebuke Satan and his imps a million times, using all the warfare scriptures that we know. Yet, God seems to turn a blind eye and a deaf ear towards us. We even threaten to backslide, but He seems to pay us no mind. At such times, it would help ease the pain a bit, if we can draw consolation in a combination of truths from the teachings of both Christ and of Peter.

> *Beloved think it not strange concerning the fiery trial which is to try you. (1 Peter 4:12). Blessed are ye when men shall revile you, and persecute you, and shall say all manner of evil against you falsely, for my sake. (Matthew 5:11). But rejoice, in as much as ye are partakers of Christ's sufferings; that, when his glory be revealed, ye may be glad also with exceeding joy. (1 Peter 4:13).*

Yes, this will be a major mark of distinction in this season of the outpouring-many will be persecuted unjustifiably for a myriad of reasons. Chief among them will be for their display of a burning passion for the presence of God, an all encompassing zeal for His house and a healthy respect for His holiness. However, may I advise you that this persecution may not always be the devil's doing? Often times it will be God at work in us. He has one item on His agenda. He wants to fast track us into mortifying the flesh (man's way of doing things), eventually releasing our spirits to mix, mingle and frolic in the surging tide of the new wine that flows from His heart to ours, in these 'times of refreshing'.

Therefore, in much the same way that the workers dance and sing, when they trample the grapes in the winepress, so too, must we continue to rejoice and sing praises unto our God in this season.

This we should do, even when it seems that everyone with a pair of size 22 military boots wants to use our lives as a hiking trail and a treadmill.

> New wine skins for new wine—the absolute necessity for Inner Healing.

In this season of the outpouring, another strong call that will echo loudly and constantly across the Body of Christ, will be the need for inner healing. In pursuit of this, it will do us well to take a closer look at the process by which wine makers, in Bible times, prepared wine skins to receive and store the new wine.

In Matthew 9:14, the disciples of John leveled scathing criticisms at Jesus for not encouraging his disciples to practice fasting, as John had taught them to do. Jesus immediately discerned their motive. He knew that they were attempting to project themselves as being holier than Peter and the other disciples of Jesus.

In his reply to them, therefore, Jesus set about shedding light on the folly of their ways. Of the three parables he used to accomplish this, the final one bears closest relevance to our discussion. It reads, "Neither do men put new wine into old bottles: else the bottles break, and the wine runneth out, and the bottles perish: but they put new wine into new bottles, and both are preserved." (Matthew 9:17).

Wrapped up in this parable is a clear message to all: To seek the increased anointing, which comes through prayer and fasting, without first seeking to heal the inner man, the true receptacle for the anointing, is to indulge in folly.

Let us, then, examine the goings-on in a typical winery of Jesus' day and see what would have prompted him to make such an observation and issue such an advisory.

In Jesus' day, wine was stored in vessels/bottles made generally of goatskin. Goatskin was most widely used because, when new, its pliability and elasticity were best suited to accommodate the volatility of the grape juice, as it matured into wine. However, as the bottles got older and the contents were used up, they would shrink and become dry, rigid and porous, if they were left to lie on a shelf for some time. This was so because goatskin is essentially leather. Leather becomes brittle, if it does not get the benefit of the moisture of the essential oils that come with polishing. Consequently, when vintage time came along and all available vessels were needed, wine makers took steps to make each unused bottle functional once again.

To accomplish this, wine makers subjected the bottles to long periods of soaking in a watery solution, in advance of the vintage season. Dissolved in this water were cleaning agents such as vinegar and salt. Submerged for so long a time, in such an environment, the bottles eventually became saturated with the solution.

The passage of the solution through the pores of the skin and its presence within the bottles not only removed stiffness and rigidity, but also sterilized them from impurities that might have accumulated while they lay idle. Thus, in one action, the pliability and elasticity of the bottles were restored. Just as significant, though, the process cleansed each bottle of impurities that would have most certainly compromised the quality of any wine stored in it.

During the time that bottles were in the water, the wine maker often tested them individually to determine their readiness for use. It was only when a bottle met the criteria of pliability and sterility that he removed it from the water to be filled with wine. Notwithstanding, even then, than bottle was not yet ready to receive the wine.

On being removed from the water, the wineskin was then taken to a room where it was glazed with a mixture of oil and butter, both inside and outside. The reason for anointing it, in this manner, was to plug the pores inherent in the goatskin. In this way, it was rendered leak-proof, ensuring that there would be no leakage, when wine was poured into it.

When the process was complete, each bottle became like new again: pliable, stretchable, clean and leak-proof. Only then did it qualify to receive and store the new wine, which was being produced m the current vintage season.

If you are spiritually sensitive, you, no doubt, have begun to see clear spiritual parallels which make this parable invaluably instructive for the prophetic season in which we are. Here is a list of some of these parallels:

- The vintage season is this season of the outpouring.
- The new wine is the anointing that comes with the outpouring of the Holy Spirit.
- The bottles or wineskins represent our inner man.
- Pliability and cleanness of the inner man are non-negotiable pre-requisites, set by God, for receipt of the anointing.
- The stiffness and rigidity of the idle wineskins are a type of what happens to Christians who do not occupy themselves with Kingdom matters. They become insensitive and stubborn concerning the will of God.
- The solution of vinegar and salt represents the soul cleansing and healing properties of the Word of God, as identified by David in Psalms 119:9 and Paul in Ephesians 5:26.
- The long waiting period in the water, in advance of the vintage season, is a type of what Isaiah recommends in Isaiah 40:31, as steps towards the renewing and strengthening of the spirit man, in advance to spiritual transformation.
- The regular testing of the wineskins to deter mine readiness for use is akin to the Lord allowing trials to come our way in his effort to turn us into fine gold.
- Anointing the skins with oil and butter to plug the pores is a type of the Lord's promise to heal our wounds in Jeremiah 30:17.
- The oil is the oil of gladness promised to those who mourn in Zion because of their wounds. (Isaiah 61).
- Butter is a concentrated form of milk. It represents the sincere milk of the Word of God, which He sends to heal our diseases. (Psalms 107:20).

Without the healing of the inner man in advance of the infilling, the child of God will experience grave frustrations. This conclusion is based on three important observations.

Firstly, according to our discussion thus far, the anointing is seen as liquid or fluid in nature. Secondly, the soul or inner man is the container for the anointing. Thirdly, whenever one is wounded, in essence, the experience in one's soul is like the puncturing of a container, leaving gaping holes in its sides. The end result is that, even though there may have been an overflow at the time of the infilling, eventually all the contents leak out, leaving the container (the inner man) empty.

It stands to reason, then, that anyone who dares to seek the anointing, without first experiencing healing of the holes in the soul, will constantly have a leakage problem. Evidence of this will be that feeling of acute spiritual dryness, even within hours of having left a worship service in which there was a tangible presence of God.

Herein lies the frustration: It is better to be in a state of hoping to be filled with the anointing than to have received the anointing and not be able to retain it. It is no wonder that one of the pervading truths that holds sway in this season advises: Whatever you obtain, you must maintain in order to retain it. Since the Lord's response is to fill anyone who hungers and thirsts after righteousness, it behooves everyone, then, to leak-proof his soul, so that he can retain the anointing that comes with the outpouring.

You may be asking, "How can I experience this healing in my inner man?" I am so glad you asked. The key to inner healing is your willingness to access forgiveness of four planes:

- Ask God to forgive you for all the sins of commission and omission, on a daily basis. This is the process called repentance that leads to and maintains your salvation. God promises to forgive you of them all. I John I: 9, NIV teaches, "If we confess our sins, he is faithful and just and will forgive us our sins and purify us from all unrighteousness."
- Forgive all the people who have hurt you. It is the only way to ensure that God forgives you. Matthew 6:14, TLB teaches, 'Your heavenly Father will forgive you if you forgive those who sin against you; but if you refuse to forgive them, he will not forgive you'. Forgive yourself. Self-condemnation

blocks the flow of God's love and that of others to you. Romans 8:1, TLB teaches, 'So there is now no condemnation awaiting those who belong to Christ Jesus.
- Forgive God. If you see God as an abuser-standing by idly while others are hurting you, it will be extremely difficult to accept His love. It is through God's love that we receive our healing. God is intrinsically good, so He can only do good. We label Him as an abuser when we ask questions such as, 'God, how come you saw all the abuse that they did to me and you did nothing?' Note well that it was only when Job forgave God that his healing process began in earnest. (Job 42).

(For a full teaching on the power of forgiveness to plug the holes in your soul and effect inner healing, I recommend my book, FORGIVENESS UNLIMITED, as mandatory reading).

"'Not by might nor by power, but by my Spirit,'
says the LORD Almighty"
(Zechariah 4:6).

By My Spirit, Says The Lord!

*A*s we bring this discourse to a close, I wish to share with you a fresh revelation that the Lord has unfolded to me out of Zechariah's vision in Zechariah 4. It paints a vivid picture of an apparatus, which depicts, in no uncertain terms, the essence of the outpouring—an unreserved release of fuel (Holy Spirit) that continuously feeds the anointing fire, so that it never goes out. Anyone who chooses to position himself before the Lord, in this season, on the same principle that the structure works, is sure to go beyond revival and live in a perpetual outpouring of the Holy Spirit. Here is an account of what Zechariah saw:

> *And (the angel) said to me, what do you see? I said, I see, and behold, a lamp stand all of gold, with its bowl (for oil) on the top of it and its seven lamps on it, and (there are) seven pipes to each of the seven lamps which are upon the top of it. (3). And there are two olive trees by it, one upon the right side of the bowl and the other upon the left side of it (feeding it continuously with oil). (Zechariah 4:2—3, AMP).*

The first notable feature of this apparatus is that it is visionary, which means that it exists in the spirit realm-outside of the reach of man's influence. This gives it prophetic significance, in that, it transcends the time in which the prophet sees it and reaches into any era in which God chooses to allow it to manifest. In that season of fulfillment, every detail concerning its structure and purpose becomes relevant to what God desires to unfold to His people. It is my humble submission that this season of the outpouring is one such season.

Zechariah identifies the apparatus as a lamp stand. Without prejudice, therefore, its purpose is to give light by way of open flame. Built into such a characteristic is a demand for the lamp stand to carry lamps that provide both the flame and a system by which the flame can be continuously fed with fuel. Based on the verse quoted above, this lamp stand does satisfy these requirements.

On this visionary lamp stand, there are seven lamps, each of which sits at the top of a set of seven pipes, which supply it with fuel. Each set of pipes is inserted into and protrudes out of a bowl filled with oil, which sits at the top of the stand. The lamp stand is strategically positioned between two olive trees, which continuously pour oil into the bowl by way of a pipe extending out of each of them into the bowl. To underscore all of this, the entire stand is made of pure gold, which calls attention to the immense value that God places on its purpose and function.

Even when considered by themselves, the features of this lamp stand do seem very striking. However, it is when compared and contrasted with those of the original, literal lamp stand, which God directed Moses to design and fabricate for the tabernacle, in the wilderness, that we see powerful, prophetic truths emerge to bring clarity and guidance for us in this season, when God wants to bring us beyond revival and into the outpouring.

Although the specifications for the lamp stand in the tabernacle were given by God, it was crafted by man, utilizing gold provided by the offerings of the people. On the other hand, the visionary lamp stand was built by God Himself, according to His will and with His own gold. How significant is this to our discourse?

The Church must accept the fact that any move of God, in the earth, is solely by God's sovereign will. If allowed to run its course, that move will grow, glow and flow as an outpouring—from a spark into a virtual inferno. In that case, we will simply be the bush upon which the self-sustaining fire of the anointing rests. However, from the moment that man believes that it is his efforts—his praying, his fasting, his prophetic declarations or his righteousness—that initiated the move and, as such, he can maintain it without continued adherence to God's updated instructions, the move declines into a revival, with a confirmed death sentence hanging over it.

The lamp stand or candlestick in the tabernacle was simply a stand or a placeholder, which provided positions on which seven lamps were placed. It comprised of six arms, three of which protruded from either side of a main shaft, which carried a groove at the top as the seventh position. It means that the lamps and the stand were separate entities. Except for holding the lamps in position, the stand contributed nothing to the quality or longevity of the flame, which burned in any given lamp.

Moreover, although the lamps rested on the same apparatus, there was no connectivity with one another. Each lamp was an end unto itself, having its own fuel on the inside. This, certainly, created the risk of compromising the quality of light that the structure gave, since, at any point in time, the flame on one or more lamps could go out because of its fuel running out. In the same vein, one or more lamps could burn brighter or dimmer than all the others, depending on the quality of fuel and the condition of the wick that provided the flame.

This is a clear picture of what goes on in a revival. There is this obvious disconnection between the ministry that is ablaze with the fire of God and the rest of the units (assemblies], even within the same denomination. This disconnectedness manifests itself in the way leaders and members of the other units of the Church think nothing of publicly leveling the most scathing criticisms against the one that is on fire.

The truth is that, although many of these leaders visit the place that is on fire, they come, not so much to fan the flames and add fuel to keep the fire alive, but to satisfy their suspicions and to collect data for justifying their predictions of a speedy death to the movement. The Brownsville experience was a case in point. One just has to log on to the respective website and one will be shocked to see the damaging predictions and reports that have been circulating, many of them purportedly written by fellow pastors of the very denomination to which the assembly belonged.

In the case of the visionary lamp stand, however, the entire apparatus was one contiguous entity-a symbol of true unity. Any attempt to separate even one lamp from the stand would have compromised the integrity of the structure.

The visionary lamp stand, itself, played an integral part in the life of the flame that burned on each lamp. It was fitted with a bowl, which acted as a reservoir from which each lamp drew fuel to sustain the flame that burned on it. In essence, then, it meant that although there were seven separate flames burning simultaneously, their light and life were of the same quality. To the eye of the beholder, the corporate light being projected by the visionary lamp stand was even. There was no lamp that outshone or that was outshone by the others—a picture of true unity.

Such is God's intention for His Church, in this season of the outpouring. In spite of what religion has tried to project, God has always seen the Church as one. Apostle Paul captures this truth very firmly in his description of the Church as the Body of Christ in 1 Corinthians 12:27, NIV: "Now you are the Body of Christ, and each one of you is a part of it."

We may each have a different function and be situated in a different locale; yet, we are all being held together by a common element—the Holy Spirit-in much the same way that the skin holds the physical body together. Additionally, just as even the remotest parts of the body are supplied with life-sustaining nutrition by blood that is pumped from the heart, so too does God intend to release, from His mouth, the same life-giving revelation to nourish the Church, even in the most far flung places of the earth.

Consequently, when God makes a sovereign move to pour out His Spirit upon us, it is not for the promoting of one assembly over the others, but for the benefit of the entire Body of Christ. The unit, at which the initial outbreak of fire occurs, serves as a catalyst for igniting a blaze throughout the entire Church. The corporate light that emanates from such a conflagration will cast an even glow over the entire earth because every ministry will be drawing its fuel from the same source—the Holy Spirit, as he is being poured out upon the Church.

According to Exodus 25, the oil used in the lamps, in the tabernacle, was a product of the olive fruit. It was obtained by crushing the olives in a press. The people would then bring it to the tabernacle as an offering unto the Lord. This means that, regard less of the extent of processing through which it passed, the oil, which was inherently pure when it was in the fruit, became subject to contamination because of microscopic impurities, suspended within it. Consequently, any lamp in which it was used, by necessity, had to be cleaned frequently, lest the inevitable accumulation of residue negatively affect its efficiency.

Moreover, since the oil for the lamp stand in the tabernacle came from the people, it is quite possible that its quantity and quality were often compromised by the way the people gave. When the people gave according to God's directives there was an adequate supply of oil. However, when they were lax, there would have been a deficit.

Such is the nature of revival. What begins as a pure move of God becomes subject to contamination and distortion, when man chooses to present offerings, to God, according to what he interprets God's will to be. If there is no realignment to God's will, by way of the cleansing of the inner man through repentance, the move loses momentum and eventually grinds to a halt.

Every day, the lamps were filled with oil and their wicks lit by a priest at sunset. They burned through the night and were extinguished, at sunrise, every morning. The fact that they had to be refilled daily was evidence of their limited capacity. This means that the flame was doomed to die as soon as the oil ran out and the disconnectedness built into the arrangement, would have cancelled any hope of one lamp being able to prolong its flame by drawing extra oil from another, close by. Does this not sound similar to the predicament of the five foolish virgins, who could get no help, when their lamps went out? Such is the nature of revival.

The wick that carried the flame was made of yarn. It had to be trimmed everyday to rid it of the portion that was burnt out during the previous night and to prepare it for fresh flames, during the night ahead. It is no wonder, then, that a tray was placed below each lamp to collect the resultant ash. Ash is symbolic of death that attends all human endeavors. Here in lies the affinity of this practice to the phenomenon known as revival.

A move of God turns into a revival and inevitably dies, when man brings his efforts to bear on the proceedings. As noble as they may be, unless they are in alignment with God's updated instructions, man's efforts will result in death and a consequent cry for the rekindling of the fire. This truth is borne out by the fact that, in any given twenty-four hour period, the lamps, a symbol of the Church, corporate and individual, had to be filled and refilled with oil, a symbol of the Holy Ghost.

It will be to our eternal advantage, if we recognize that our inherent limitations will always prevent us from retaining the infilling of the Holy Spirit by our own efforts. We must maintain our connection to God. Without that connection, the anointing fire will soon go out, regardless of how intensely it burns initially

Within that same period, the flames, a symbol of the anointing fire, had to be kindled and rekindled on each lamp. Just as it obtains in a revival the fire ignites, rages for a while, then it dies and very soon we are asking for God to set us on fire once more. Oh, how the Father wishes that we would retain the fire that He gives us by taking steps to maintain it, in accordance with His will.

In addition to this, the wicks, a symbol of man immersed in the anointing and ablaze for God, had to be trimmed, regularly. You see, although the anointing fire comes from God, because the basic nature of man's efforts add up to being nothing but wood, hay and stubble, man becomes subject to burnout, which is one of the veritable killers of any move of God.

Moreover, the fact that the entire operation rested on the shoulders of man (the priest) for its efficiency and function, it gave rise to the possibility of a breakdown at some point. This could have been due to neglect, complacency and/or lack of diligence to duty.

It is inherent in even the most vigilant and anointed of us to make slip-ups, from time to time.

A strong case in point emerges out of the incident with Nadab and Abihu, sons of Aaron in Leviticus 10:1&2. As priests, they were duty bound to adhere strictly to the rules that governed the burning of incense, at the altar in the tabernacle. However, they allowed their human frailties, such as presumption, lack of diligence and craving for public accolade to drive them into offering strange fire before the Lord. For this they died at the door of the tent of meeting.

If it were so, then, the possibility exists that there might have been many an evening when the lighting of the lamps was either late or not efficiently done because of human failing. Such is the nature of revival—the life and quality of a move of God becomes compromised because human beings fall short in their shouldering of responsibility to keep the fire going

However, when we contrast the set of features cited above, with corresponding features of the visionary lamp stand, we see a completely different picture. The truth is that what we are beholding is the perfect picture of the Church, corporate and individual, caught in the all-encompassing, ever expanding, ever-intensifying conflagration that the anointing generates. It is truly fascinating.

Earlier, we alluded to the fact that the entire visionary lamp stand is the epitome of unity. Unlike the one, in the tabernacle, which was simply a place holder for seven lamps that were separate from each other, all the components of this lamp stand are joined into one unit. Although there are seven individual lamps, they are all connected to the same bowl from which they draw oil for the flame that each of them carries. Such an arrangement means that each lamp burns at the same level of intensity and brightness and carries equivalent potential for longevity. None rivals the other for supremacy. They truly operate in one accord. Does this not sound familiar?

Unity is both a prerequisite for the onset of the outpouring and a vital element in its maintenance. Wherever it exists, one sees a mirror image of the outpouring in operation. One such situation is Psalms 133, which credits unity with the power to:

- Create an atmosphere of goodness and congeniality—the ideal setting for genuine worship; pursuit of the heart of God and teamwork, all of which are indicators of the existence of the outpouring in a given locale.
- Generate a flow of anointing oil—a symbol of the Holy Spirit who fuels the anointing fire and directs operations during the outpouring.
- Cause the oil (anointing) to flow from the head of Aaron (the designated leader) - to his beard (those appointed to serve with the leader)—to his skirts (the general congregation). The oil flowing from Aaron's head-a central point-to the rest of his body compares favorably with the oil flowing from the bowl to the lamps on the lamp stand.
- Produce dew or a fresh experience daily, which is the essence of the outpouring.
- Attract the blessings of the Lord, which provides ample evidence of the outpouring upon an individual or corporate body.

I challenge you to do an analysis of other scriptures that celebrate the virtues of unity. I guarantee that you will be able to identify within them elements which capture the essence of the visionary lamp stand, as it pertains to the mechanics upon which the wheels of the outpouring turn. Let me give you a jumpstart with two of them.

- Acts 2, which begins with evidence that unity attracts the anointing fire and ends with proof that, as long as unity is maintained, the fire never goes out. It simply mutates itself into prophetic preaching, divine favor, genuine fellowship and consistent numerical growth. John 15, which reiterates the fact that, as long as we stay connected to/united with Jesus, the vine, there will be a continuous flow of the pure wine of the Spirit into our inner man. It is that wine, which infuses into us the Zoë life of God, nourishing our spirits and fortifying us to repel the inevitable, vicious attacks on the outpouring.

Notice that the oil, which fuels the flames on the visionary lamp stand, comes into the bowl, not by way of extraction from the olive fruit, but by way of direct input from the two olive trees positioned on either side of it. One must remember that it is not necessarily the olive fruit, but rather, the olive tree that is the primary producer of oil. An olive is simply a container within which the tree stores its oil, in a form that makes it accessible to whoever is willing to put out the effort to extract it. As indicated previously, regardless of the intricacy of the extraction/filtration system, the fact that the olive has to be crushed to extract the oil, presupposes that the final product is intrinsically loaded with residual particles. Any lamp in which this oil is used will have to be cleaned regularly because of a buildup of residue, over time. That greatly hampers its ability to burn efficiently and brightly.

By deduction, therefore, the insertion of the pipes directly into the olive trees to stimulate a flow of oil into the bowl is symbolic of drawing the anointing directly from God, the true source. Such a move dispenses with the possibility of human inefficiency as it pertains to the supply of oil to the bowl, eliminates any possibility of residual impurities and ensures a perpetual supply of pure, unadulterated oil.

In essence, this is the basic chemistry that flows at the very heart of the outpouring: God, by His sovereign authority, releases His Spirit upon all who position themselves, with the correct disposition, where the shower is falling or the river is flowing. Since God is essentially pure, that which comes out of Him is also pure.

It stands to reason, then, that every genuine move of God begins pure. As long as He continues to be the source of the flow, the director of operations and the central focus of all involved, that move of God naturally gathers momentum and magnitude over time, until the Holy Spirit showers down upon and saturates all flesh.

No human being must lay claim to the outpouring-neither to its origin nor to its sustenance-lest his inherent imperfections seep in and compromise its purity. Everyone must know that the outpouring comes not because of our months of fasting and prayer, spirited praise and worship or by our sorrowful repentance and efforts at being righteous. These human activities simply signal to God that we are developing a disposition to obey His will. Moreover, similar to Moses' experience, they effectively turn us into and position us as the bush from which God spoke to Moses, in the back side of the desert. When we are in position or in correct alignment with His will, God comes down and rests upon us as the only Self-sustaining, Consuming Fire.

It is important to note, as well that unlike what took place in the tabernacle, none of the lamps carries a wick, yet, there is a flame, burning intensely on each of them. You see, a wick eventually burns out, causing the flame, burning upon it, to die la means, then, that each flame is burning on raw fuel that comes from within the lamp itself. This is clear indication that, as long as there is fuel in the lamp (and that is always) the flame can never go out. It is somewhat like that which obtains in an oil refinery where there is a stack on which excess fuel, emitted by the refining process, is burnt. As long as petroleum is being processed, which is continuously, the fire does not go out.

Bearing in mind that the wick is also symbolic of man immersed in the anointing and that man is subject to burnout, its absence from the visionary lamp stand is evidence of God's desire to eliminate ideas, doctrines, philosophies and theologies of human origin from the equation that results in the initiation and retention of the outpouring. God wants the out pouring to be His doing—His fire, burning on raw anointing, supplied by His Spirit. In such a case, the human being is not the director of operations during the outpouring. Rather, he is granted the awesome privilege of partnering with God, in His quest to make the knowledge of His glory, "cover the earth, as the waters cover the sea." (Habakkuk 2:14).

Since partnership is built on the principles of shared responsibilities and shared resources, man stands to benefit immensely anytime he chooses to partner with God. Note, though, that in this case shared does not mean equal. You see, in reality, we do not bring much to the table except for our obedience and willingness. God is the one who owns everything. (Psalms 24:1). It means, then, that, as long as we are willing to partner with God to initiate, maintain and cause to expand an outpouring of the Spirit,

He will give us the good of the land. (Isaiah 1:19). It is no wonder, therefore, that wherever the outpouring is taking place, there is a marked increase in finances and material wealth among God's people.

Another aspect of the visionary lamp stand that bears great significance for us, in this season of the outpouring, is the fact that the number of lamps, as well as the number of the pipes that feed each of them, is seven. This compares favorably with the vision that John saw in Revelation 1:12-16—seven golden lamp stands with Jesus standing in the middle. Without begging the question, there must also be some affinity between these and Isaiah's prophecy, concerning the sevenfold anointing with which Jesus would minister, in Isaiah 11:2, NIV:

> The Spirit of the Lord will rest on him—the Spirit of wisdom and of understanding, the Spirit of counsel and of power; the Spirit of knowledge and of the fear of the Lord.

Notice that the number seven is the common element, linking the three references cited above. In scripture, seven is a symbol of perfection, completeness, wholeness, totality and perpetuity. The seven armed lamp stand of Zechariah is representative of the outpouring. By way of Jesus' own interpretation, the seven golden lamp stands of Revelation are figurative of the Church. The sevenfold anointing of Isaiah is characteristic of Holy Spirit who is both the fuel for the outpouring and the executive director of the Church.

Accordingly, another major truth, pertaining to the anatomy of the outpouring, emanates out of these facts: When God pours out His Spirit upon an assembly, His aim is to have that assembly act as a fountain (bowl) from which the Church, in its totality, can draw on an anointing that continually pushes it into perfect alignment with His will. In pursuit of this, the Holy Spirit releases revelation that updates our knowledge of Kingdom truths, and provides us with wisdom and understanding to apply them to our lives. The cumulative effect of all of this is an infusion of power into the

Church, both corporate and individual, to project a clear picture of Jesus, the one who stands in the midst of his Church.

Yes, this is God's definitive intent for every move that He initiates in His Church-He wants to bring healing to the broken, hurting members of the Body of Christ and to draw the diverse parts of the Church into one complete whole. It is only then that the world will see the real Jesus about whom we preach so loudly, standing in the midst of us.

You see, no single individual or assembly or denomination can truthfully claim to have the fullness of the image of Christ. Like in the Sci-fi movies, it takes the coming together of all the parts, each one made whole and ablaze with the glory, in its own right, to generate the power to create and project the real Christ, in all his glory. When this happens, God's glorious image will hover over the Church, for always, just as it did over the tabernacle, in the wilderness by way of the glory cloud in the day and the pillar of fire by night.

Within the Church, the oil that flows out of such a state of unity will nullify any hint of friction that personality conflict may bring. The doxa—the totality of God wrapped up in His glory—will be evident by the manifestation of God's splendor, character, beauty and strength in the lives of His people. The kabod—the weightiness or authority of God—will manifest itself by way of signs, wonders and miracles. The shekinah—the dimension of God's glory within which He communes with His people, when they are in one accord (Exodus 25:22)—will beckon us into His throne room for sweet fellowship with Him. As we emerge out of the throne room, the qaran—the shooting rays of glory, as what shone on Moses' face—will be irrefutable evidence that we have come face to face with God in His majestic glory. The impact on the world will be phenomenal.

The world will cringe to see the Church marching forward as one unit. We will no longer be the laughing stock of the print and electronic media because of the indisputable proof of the new authority, dignity and power with which we are conducting our affairs. They will not be able to deny us entry into and having a significant say in politics, economics, higher education or business, as the Joel 2 principle finally kicks in. Truly, we will let our light shine so that men will see and acknowledge the good workmanship that the Father is carrying out upon us. Yes, they will see the image of Jesus, firmly etched on the Church, for all times, and will glorify our Father in heaven. And that, in essence, is the absolute divinely ordained purpose for the outpouring.

Now let us take a more in-depth look at the two olive trees and see what further outpouring-related inferences, we can draw. Let us be reminded of the scenario: There is a lamp stand, fitted with a bowl. There are two olive trees, one standing on either side of it, continuously pouring oil into the bowl. Attached to and inserted into the bowl are seven lamps, which draw oil from it to feed the fame, burning on each of them. Again, considering this lamp stand and the mechanics upon which it works as being symbolic of the Church caught up in the outpouring, here are a few of the inferences that we can draw. They will fascinate us, to say the least.

Positioning is everything

The lamp stand, standing between the two olive trees, is figurative of the absolute need for us to be properly positioned in this season of the outpouring. Where I am will determine what I receive from God.

There are a few basic questions we must answer, when seeking to correctly position ourselves to maximize what God is offering in this season.

- How equipped is the ministry with which I am affiliated to help me discover, pursue and fulfill my destiny?
- Is there a strong enough anointing flowing in that place to handle the situations that confront me? If I cannot get honest answers to both of these questions, I must move on to a place that does.
- How prepared am I mentally, psychologically and spiritually to bloom where I am planted, for the season that I am there, even in the face of great odds?

- How disposed am I to obey God when He instructs me to move from one place to another? Can I defy the power of sentimentality that is known to sentence people to die in dry places?
- Do I have the fortitude to do what God says in spite of public opinion?
- How responsive am I to the new things of God?

Apostolic and Prophetic Anointing

The two olive trees represent the role of the apostolic and prophetic anointing in keeping alive the fire that comes with the outpouring. Through the prophetic anointing, God feeds the fire with fresh revelation. This fits firmly into the framework of Moses' admonition to Israel, in Deuteronomy 8:3,NLT, "people need more than bread for their life; real life comes by feeding on every word of the Lord." By way of the apostolic anointing, God infuses into the Church divine authority to work miracles, signs and wonders and to take control over territorial spirits.

This is the reason that God has reintroduced the offices of the Apostle and the Prophet into the Church in this season. In fact one of the tell tale signs of the outpouring is the empowering of the sons and daughters of God to prophesy. You see, Apostles and Prophets are layers of strong foundation in the Church. It is well known that regardless of how large and spectacular the superstructure looks, certain disaster will befall any building for which a strong foundation has not been laid.

Working under the principle of continuity, Apostles carry an anointing to father ministries and mentor leaders who are designated to take the Church into and safely through ensuing cycles of divine release. Prophets are the eyes of the Church that bring enlightenment to the Body of Christ, so that we all would know which way to go. Can the Church risk not having the Apostles and Prophets release their anointing into it? I think not.

Praise and Worship

The two olive trees, pouring pure oil continuously into the bowl, speak of the high value that God places on praise and worship, as instruments for generating the atmosphere most conducive for bringing in and maintaining His presence. Psalms 22:3 informs us that God enthrones Himself in the praises of His people.

Revelations 4 reveals that worship is the correct posture that we should adopt, when we come before God, seated on His throne, in glorious majesty. The truth is that heaven is as powerful, prosperous and impregnable as it is, because it is empowered by praise and worship. It stands to reason, then, that any individual or ministry that engages in Spirit-led praise and passionate, truth-filled worship of God will experience heaven on earth before leaving earth to go to heaven.

When we stand to praise and worship God, we actually create a graphic reflection of the lamp stand, standing between the two olive trees. Our hands lifted up are the pipes or, to update it to the level of modern day technology, the satellite dish that downloads the anointing which is being poured out from the heart of God. Our inner man—soul and spirit-becomes the bowl, into which the anointing flows, creating a reservoir of supernatural power that can perpetually fuel our march to divine destiny and purpose. Any individual or assembly that makes it a practice to truly praise the Lord with joy and worship him in spirit and in truth will be well set to glow continuously with God's glory. This is the essence of the outpouring.

Fruits and Gifts

The two olive trees are an expression of the balance that the Church must strike between the yearning for the gifts of the Spirit and the divine mandate to display the fruit of the Spirit. I call it the battle between charisma and character.

Charisma is God's gift to man but character is man's gift to God. The person or ministry that strikes the correct balance between them is guaranteed to lead a fruitful and prosperous existence that only gets better, as it impacts one generation after another. However, when more energies are expended in the pursuit of the gifts than in the development of sound, Christ-like character, the inevitable excesses bring pain and shame to all concerned and cause the anointing fire to go out, with little hope of it being rekindled, in many cases.

It is for the purpose of striking proper balance that God inspired Apostle Paul to strategically position his treatise on love—the embodiment of the fruit of the Spirit (Galatians 5:22) and the foundation of sound character-in i Corinthians 13, directly between 1 Corinthians 12, in which he details the gifts of the Spirit and 1 Corinthians 14, in which he pinpoints prophesy as the best gift to choose. What a brilliant piece of literary engineering on the part of Apostle Paul!

It reiterates, emphatically, what Jesus admonishes his disciples, in John 13:35, NIV, "By this all men will know that you are my disciples, if you love one another." For Christ, the Master Builder of the Church and the initiator of the outpouring, neither the spectacular display of the power gifts nor the pinpoint accuracy of the utterance gifts, in any way, convey the true picture of who we are supposed to be. As far as Christ is concerned, love for one another is the only item of importance on our Kingdom Identification Card.

The King/Servant Principle

At Divine Destiny Worship Centre, Trinidad, West Indies, the ministry for which God has given me direct responsibility, we regularly make this proclamation, which we call our Destiny Statement: To become God's treasured possession in the earth empowered to rule, yet, willing to serve.

At first glance, this statement seems to be quite oxymoronic, from the point of view that ruler ship is hardly ever equated with servant hood. Yet, it is an apt description of one of the heaviest mandates that God has placed upon His Church. The truth is that the principle, which it espouses, formed part of the core of Jesus' teachings to his disciples, while he was in the earth and remains at the very heart of the character of the Church that he is building, today.

In his attempt to settle frequent disputes among his disciples, on the question of who would be the greatest or the ruler among them, Jesus would often declare to them, "But he that is greatest among you shall be your servant." (Matthew 23:11, KJV). By this, Jesus was embedding into the very foundation of the Church, the King/Servant principle, which God established for us, since the beginning.

In Genesis 1:28, God gave us dominion over the earth. He then turns around and sets us in Eden to work/serve. Later on, He told Moses that His expressed intent for bringing Israel out of Egypt was to reactivate the original King/Servant mandate. He would accomplish this by transforming them from being a band of slaves into becoming a Kingdom of priests (Exodus 19:2-6). Many years later, Apostle Peter, first Pastor of the Church, repeated the same sentiments, when he described the Church as "a royal priesthood'. (Peter 2: 9).

Yes, every child of God must note that the anointing, which comes with the outpouring empowers us with supernatural authority. Yet, we must never lose sight of the truth that such an infusion of power does not make the recipient greater than those around him. Rather, it obliges him to become a servant to all, seeing that he is merely a channel of the anointing and not the Anointed One. To do any less will be to set oneself up for a devastating blackout and the clogging of the pipes through which the anointing flows. Our fervent prayer should be, therefore: 'Lord, in this season of the outpouring, I seek you, not only for the power to rule over sickness and circumstances, but also, for a servant's heart, so that I can become my brother's keeper.

Oil and Wine

One of the main reasons for the Samaritan being able to help the wounded man on the road to Jericho was the fact that he carried oil and wine with him. (Luke 10:30–36). He, himself, had come to appreciate these two elements as a winning combination for bringing healing to the wounds inflicted on him by abusive Jewish neighbors, on an almost daily basis. Consequently, he never went anywhere without them, just in case he would meet someone who needed healing.

God knows that in this season of the outpouring, there is always the possibility of soldiers being wounded from the relentless attacks which Satan will launch, in his attempt to short circuit the move of God. In anticipation, He is again releasing oil and wine into the Church to bring healing to the wounded and restoration to the fallen. The oil stands for the anointing that destroys yokes and removes burdens. Wine represents the joy factor, which brings renewed strength, so that the fallen can soar again.

When oil and wine are properly mixed and applied in the correct dosage, there is no room for character assassination, condemnation and self-righteousness. Rather, there is an overflow of compassion that draws one to the fallen and the wounded, even at the risk of getting one's own name sullied. In that case, love becomes a stronger power than self-preservation.

The Church must remember that one of the enemy's strategies is to strike the shepherd, hoping that the sheep will scatter. Consequently, we must be prepared to restore key leaders who may become primary targets for the onslaught of the enemy, in this season. If we fail to let the oil and wine flow, the outpouring can become a trickle, bringing the move of God to a screeching halt, for lack of experienced, anointed leadership. Why not open up your spirit and receive the oil and wine from Holy Spirit, RIGHT NOW! Declare, "I RECEIVE IT!"

Faith and Works

Earlier, I alluded to the fact that, when we pray, God does answer prayer, but not always in the form and manner that we expect. His preferred way is to release answers wrapped up in a set of instructions. The one who is willing to follow the instructions, step by step, will see the answer to his prayer gradually emerge in plain view.

The bottom line is that God never intended prayer to be a faith-only exercise. He always expected us, in the earth, to take appropriate action, in anticipation of receiving the answer that he has already prepared in the heavens. Simply sitting around, expecting God to do everything for us, under the guise of exercising faith, is nothing but foolishness. It will get us nowhere, except deeper and deeper into frustration. Faith must be accompanied by works (James 2:17).

It is no wonder; therefore, that there was such outrage at the ridiculous extremes to which people went, during the mid-1900's, when the Word of Faith Movement was on. Many leaders, as well as members of the Body of Christ died, unnecessarily, because they refused to accept medical treatment. Their philosophy was that to do so would constitute a lack of faith in God. My question, on this issue, still begs for an answer: If accepting medical attention is sinful, can doctors who give it get saved? Needless to say, what God intended to last from generation to generation, petered out into nothingness.

In this season of the outpouring, we must not make the same mistakes. God is releasing deep revelation of His word into the Church, so that we can build strong faith to work miracles, heal the sick, raise the dead and attract divine favor. However, He is making a simultaneous infusion of wisdom and understanding to make His people more action oriented. Consider these two gems for victorious living:

- Those things which are not will only become things that are, when we take the action to make them what they are supposed to be.
- We can only possess what we confess, if we pass the-turn-faith-into-works test.

The Latter House Will Be More Glorious

It is through Prophet Haggai, a contemporary of Zechariah, that God sends a message of hope to Zerubbabel, governor of Judah, to Joshua, the High Priest, and to the people of Judah, as a whole. The message, in part, reads thus:

> *The latter glory of this house (with its successor, to which Jesus came) shall be greater than the former, says the Lord of hosts; and in this place will I give peace and prosperity, says the Lord of hosts (Haggai 2:9, AMP).*

What powerful words of encouragement for a people who were becoming increasingly frustrated because of seemingly insurmountable opposition from their detractors! They had only recently returned to Jerusalem, after some seventy years in exile and were determined to rebuild the temple, which had been lying in ruin all that time. However, their detractors had succeeded in placing obstacles of every imaginable type in their way. The cumulative effect of the attacks had generated such deep discouragement among the people that they had withdrawn their labor, leaving the project grossly incomplete.

It is in this context that God now sends Prophet Haggai. He brings a message geared towards generating hope and stimulating the people to rise up and put the finishing touches to the house of God. The central theme of the message is this: "Regardless of how depressing things may look at the moment, the temple will not only be rebuilt, but also, it will be more glorious than the one King Solomon had built."

What Haggai has delivered, in words, God now gives to Zechariah, in vision. In reality, then, the lamp stand, which Zechariah sees, is symbolic of the visual effect that the completed temple will have on those who see it. Since we have also been pitching the visionary lamp stand as a type of the Church, ablaze with the fire of the outpouring, we will not be begging the question at all, to proclaim that Haggai's prophecy continues to resonate, even in our time: The glory of the Church, in this season of the out pouring, will be far greater than that of the Church, in any era, since its inauguration in the Upper Room. What an exciting prospect to look forward to!

The justification for such a claim is founded on the answer that the angel gives to Zechariah, when he asks for an explanation of the vision. The angel skillfully uses the visionary lamp stand as a projector through which he casts a detailed picture of the process that must play itself out to bring Haggai's message to pass. Let us examine the angel's picture one frame at a time and see its relevance to Judah in Zechariah's day and to the Church in this season of the outpouring

> *"You will succeed, not by military might or by your own strength, but by my spirit." (Zechariah 4:6, TEV).*

God assures the leaders of Judah that they will be successful in completing the project. However, He warns them not to count on military might and strategic planning to bring it about. They will have to rely on the guidance of and empowerment by the Holy Spirit.

The admonition is the same for us today. For any move of God to escape the death grip of the revival syndrome, we will have to let Holy Spirit become the coach who calls the play, one scene at a time. In response, we will pull together as a team, triggering a perpetual flow of the anointing oil that will cause us to transcend into the ever-intensifying, ever-expanding consuming fire of the outpouring. Then, our spirited praise, solemn worship, mournful repentance, extravagant giving and days of national, regional and global prayer will make sense.

> *"For who are you, O great mountain of human obstacles)? Before Zerubbabel...you shall become a plain (a mere molehill)!" (Zechariah 4:7, AMP).*

When the Holy Spirit takes control of operations, he confronts our enemies on our behalf. Like he did with Jehoshaphat (2

Chronicles 20), he makes both us and our enemies know that the battle is no longer ours but his.

Can you imagine the impact such a turn of events will have on the systems of the world, today? Politicians, journalists, financiers, and even religious leaders who have prided themselves with being responsible for retarding the progress of the Church, will finally find themselves having to contend with an entity that packs forward moving power like a giant steamroller, coming down a hill, having neither driver nor brakes. Stop that if you can, devil!

Yes, the outpouring is God's secret strategy for empowering the Church to walk in the original dimension of power and authority that Jesus programmed into it, the instant that Peter received the revelation of him as the Christ (Matthew 16:18). The Church, ablaze with the fire of the outpouring, will steamroll its way through the gates of hell. It will flatten every obstacle standing against it. And there will not be a thing that hell can do about it. So, look out world and hell alike, here comes the Church on fire!

> *"The hands of Zerubbabel have laid the foundations of this house; his hands shall also finish it." (Zechariah 4:9).*

The outpouring carries a finisher's anointing within it. Anyone who gets caught up in its wake is suddenly overcome by a strong passion for tying up loose ends in his life and bringing unfinished business to completion.

Hence the reason in ministries, where the rivers of the outpouring are flowing, people go back to school to obtain that diploma or degree, the pursuit of which they had abandoned many years before. The Zerubbabels (Leaders) of these ministries seem to get renewed vigor to pursue and accomplish the dimensions of the vision, which they had been forced to shelve because of lack of human and financial resources.

The finisher's anointing is an integral element in the profile of Christ, the Master Builder of the Church and the director of operations during the outpouring. Hebrews 12:2 labels him as the Alpha and Omega, the Author and the Finisher of our faith.

Although in the building of the Church, he has had to contend with hindrances from all quarters, Christ is determined to finish the job and do it with great flare. He will prepare and present to himself a glorious Church without spot or wrinkle (Ephesians 5:26, KJV).

If, in its infancy, as recorded in the book of Acts, the Church created such a stir and imposed its influence on world affairs so authoritatively, can you imagine what it will do when Christ is finished with it? If in its infancy, it became enveloped in such glory can you envisage the intensity of the greater glory that will shroud us?

Note well that there is an explosive glory that comes from finishing, which one does not see at the beginning. Truly the latter house will be more glorious than the former. As we take our rightful place in the arenas of human endeavor, without prejudice, the earth will be filled with the knowledge of the glory of God. Consider this gem for victorious living and make it your personal credo:

The finisher's anointing is upon me. I am a finisher; not a dropout!

> *"Who (with reason) despises the day of small things?"*
> *(Zechariah 4:10, AMP).*

Large religious bodies, both Christian and non Christian, have long looked on us, the body of true believers in Christ, with disdain and have labeled us as 'small church' people. Their collective mindset seems to be that we are only of nuisance value—there, only to point out sin, corruption, violation of human rights and the absolute need for reliance on God. As far as they are concerned, we, the Church, have very little of worth to contribute to the advancement of society. The only time that they seem to pay any real attention to us is when there is some negative incident, which they may use to criticize the Church in the press and on talk shows for weeks on end.

However, allow me to respond to them by using a cliché in vogue today, 'Enough is enough!' The world is in for a big surprise. The ridicule has gone on for too long. This outpouring, which God is releasing upon the Church, is generating an intensity of divine glory within its bowels. Soon, radiance will burst forth from within the Church. It will drive fear into the movers and shakers of this world. It will be a repetition of what happened in the wilderness, on every occasion that Moses returned from meeting with God face to face on the mountain—the garan or shooting glory radiated from his face with such intensity that Aaron and the rest of the people had to run and hide from him. Then, we can proclaim Psalms 27:1-2, TEV:

The Lord is my light and my salvation; I will fear no one....2. When evil men attack me and try to kill me, they stumble and fall.

Yes, the Church will be a force for the world to reckon with. Those who sit in the commanding heights of the systems by which the world is governed will not be able to ignore us anymore. The financiers will no longer have the opportunity to humiliate men and women of God who are in the market for funding, acquisition or expansion of property for ministry. God's people will have finally learnt how to buy into the vision of their leaders. Ministries will be erecting huge complexes either debt free or with minimal financing from those institutions.

Can any good thing come out of the Church? I say, a thousand times, "YES! Just wait and see!" The Church needs to know that and the world needs to take note of it as well. Therefore, to the Church, I echo the prophetic words of Isaiah, as found in Isaiah 60:1, AMP:

> ARISE (from the depression and prostration in which circumstances have kept you—rise to a new life)! Shine (be radiant with the glory of the Lord), for your light has come, and the glory of the Lord has risen upon you!

In the same vein, I deliver this advisory to the rulers of this world, 'Make way for the Church, because "the least one shall become a thousand (a clan), and the small one a strong nation. I, the Lord, will hasten it in its (appointed) time.' (Isaiah 60:22, AMP).

> *"For these seven lamps represent the eyes of the Lord that see everywhere around the world." (Zechariah 4:10, TLB).*

We have already established by way of revelation that the seven lamps on the visionary lamp stand rep resent the end-time Church caught up in the blaze of the outpouring. Now, here comes another angle of interpretation, from the lips of the angel, himself. He explains to Zechariah that the seven lamps rep resent the eyes of the Lord that see all around the world.

When we put these two streams of revelation together we see emerging a most formidable image of the Church, as it will impact world affairs, in these last days. Let us bring the curtains down on this discourse by identifying the dynamics of the Church functioning as the eyes of the Lord and the implications of fulfilling such a role.

The Church is the eyes of God

As we determined earlier, seven represents fullness, completeness or universality. It means, then, that the Church, symbolized by the seven lamps, is mandated to provide God with omni vision—the ability to see everything, everywhere, at the same time. Hence the reason God is determined to establish the Church in every corner of the globe, before the end of this age.

Jesus prophesied, in Matthew 24:14, that the gospel of the Kingdom will be preached everywhere as a witness to all mankind before the end comes. Wherever the gospel is preached it becomes the power of God that brings people to salvation. All who receive salvation become part of the Church to which Christ has given the keys of the Kingdom of God to bring the powers of hell under the authority of Heaven. We are now equipped to open and lock gates of power in the atmosphere of the earth, according to the will of God.

One such gate is the eye or vision gate. He wants to peer into every area of activity in which mankind is involved. 2 Chronicles 16:9, TLB, informs us that 'the eyes of the Lord search back and forth across the whole earth, looking for people whose hearts are perfect toward him, so that he can show his great power in helping them.' Proverbs 15:3, KJV, further states that 'the eyes of the Lord are in every place, beholding the evil and the good.'

The Church is God's Witness

Jesus told his disciples in Acts 1:8, that, after the Holy Spirit is poured out upon them, they will be his witnesses throughout the earth. Traditionally, in our effort to carry out this mandate, the Church has sent out teams of people to give out tracts in the neighborhood, in shopping malls and on street corners. We have held cottage meetings, street meetings and crusades, seeking to win souls for Jesus. These are all legitimate activities in our response to the great commission and have yielded tremendous results. Have we ever considered, though, that being a witness for Jesus may involve more than these activities?

Literally a witness is one who provides evidence in the defense or prosecution of an accused person in court. The key prerequisite, however, is that he must prove that he saw or was an eye witness to the incident in question. If all he has is hearsay evidence, his credibility comes into question and he may be disqualified.

It means, then, that the Church, in pursuit of its role as the eyes of the Lord, must formulate ways of infiltrating major institutions and systems of this world to gather evidence of the goings-on to bring them before God. We must be abreast of changes and trends in politics, economics, law, crime, religion, just to name a few. Having gathered such evidence, we, then come to the court of intercession and present them before God, imploring Him to reward, forgive, heal or punish, according to His will.

Another function of a witness is that of being a representative of another person or institution. He is a veritable ambassador, virtually walking in the same authority and possessing the same abilities as the one whom he represents. This is exciting news for the Church.

The release of the outpouring upon us, in this season, is geared towards enduing us with exousia, dumamis and energia power from Holy Spirit.

- Equipped with exousia power, we will fit the role of true ambassadors for Christ. We will speak with the authority of Heaven. We will apply the power of the anointing to destroy

yokes and remove burdens that have been imposed upon mankind and the earth, itself, by unscrupulous leaders and unjust systems. We will proudly pro claim the Kingdoms of the earth to become the Kingdoms of our God.
- Endued with dunamis power, we will work the very works that Jesus wrought, while he was in the earth. Miracles, signs and wonders will be the order of the day in every place where the Church is planted, as a witness of the God that lives and works in us.
- Empowered by energia power, we will operate like the proverbial 'Energizer Bunny –We will just keep on going and going and going. Like Jeremiah, the word of God will set off an internal combustion engine within us. By this, we will be energized in our physical bodies and mental faculties to match the passion in our spirits for the pursuit of our divine purpose and destiny.

The Church is God's Watchman

According to scripture, a watchman is a Prophet or a Seer. He has the unique privilege of peering into the spirit world to see things on behalf of God and people. God gives the watchman understanding of what he sees and of the times within which he lives. Then, God mandates the watchman to proclaim His mind on the issues, which he has seen, so that the people will know what to do. Therefore, since the Church is the eyes of the Lord who beholds the good and the evil of this world, it stands to reason that we must have answers for the vexing questions that continue to gnaw away at the very fabric of what constitutes life, today.

We can no longer turn a blind eye against the happenings around us. Neither can we nonchalantly renege on our responsibility to watch after the welfare of the souls of men, in the face of gross exploitation and distortion of truth. The anointing that is now upon us will drive us out of our comfort zone and land us right in the middle of controversy, pertaining to matters such as abortion, homosexuality, terrorism, criminal justice, and civil rights, just to name a few.

However, our approach will not be along the lines of the world's system. You will not see us with placards, marching in rowdy mobs through the streets. We will take the approach of:

- Closing ranks in unity.
- Repairing or establishing strong interpersonal relationships.
- Repenting on behalf of and rededicating ourselves, our families, our communities and our nations to God.
- Attacking and subduing the spiritual forces—principalities, powers, rulers of the darkness of this world and spiritual wickedness in high places that control men, systems and territories.
- Announcing the truth of God's word, concerning every issue. pronouncing the judgment of God upon institutions and the people that run them, if they refuse to yield to the will of God.
- Proclaiming to both the Church and the world at large that our time of jubilee-God-ordained freedom—has come.

Like the watchman in Isaiah 21:11 those who are anointed to see and speak on God's behalf will finally peel off the muzzle that has been imposed upon us by the press and electronic media. Even in the face of irrefutable evidence of corruption and immorality on the part of leaders of the Church, we will yet open our mouths and declare what we see. The rest of the world, totally confused about the goings-on, will be asking, "Watchman, what of the night? Watch man, what of the night?" But we, the watchers, will gladly proclaim, "Arise, shine for your light has come and the glory of the Lord is rising up in you! You have been weeping all through a long, difficult night, because of your oppressors. But there is no need to give up hope. God has heard your cry and He has come down to set you free. The dawning of a new day is here and it will bring you joy unspeakable and the fullness of God's glory!"

So come on Church, it is time to climb up into the watchtower and take a look at the horizon. There is a tsunami of God's glory rolling in. When you catch sight of it, open your mouth and declare what you see. God wants us to be the watchmen that will shed light on the puzzling events that are casting ominous shadows across the landscape of people's minds.

The Church is God's Lighthouse

In the days before the advent of satellite tracking systems and computers, the captains of ships depended heavily on the lighthouses, strategically located along the shoreline for safe navigation into the harbor. In fact, it is said that by virtue of the powerful beams of light with which they lit up the dark skies and black seas, these lighthouses were the virtual eyes that captains used to see their way through the treacherous reefs and narrow channels that led to the berths alongside the pier. Even so, is the role of the Church in today's darkened world.

The Church is under a heavy obligation to shed light along the pathway of life so that people will make it safely through the mazes that dot the journey from the womb to the tomb and into eternity. Ours is the very mission that Jesus willingly accepted in Luke 4:18—to preach the gospel. The gospel consists basically of the word of God.

David writes Psalms 119, his longest Psalm, in celebration of the virtues that the word of God has instilled in his life. In Psalms 119:105, he testifies that he uses the word as a lantern with which to negotiate the dark patches along the pathway to destiny. In Psalms 119:130, he proclaims that wherever the word of God is preached, it brings forth light. In Psalms 119:133, David implores the Lord to please use His word to establish order in the way he walks.

It should not be difficult to conclude, therefore, that as long as the Church is faithful in delivering the gospel to the ends of the earth, a pathway will always be opened for:

- The poor to see their way out of poverty.

- The brokenhearted to receive the good news that the pieces of their heart will be put back together.
- The captives to be delivered out of bondage and empowered to take the freedom walk.
- The eyes of the blind to be opened to see which way they should go.
- Those that are bruised to be liberated from the debilitating effects of the poisons, secreted by roots of bitterness—the cumulative effect of abuse.
- All and sundry to hear the exciting announcement that they are entitled to a season of jubilee—freedom from debt on all fronts.

It is no surprise, then, that in this season of the outpouring, God is enriching the content of the revealed word which He is downloading to the Church. The operative principle seems to be that the richer the content of the word that flows into the Church, it is the greater the intensity with which the Church, in its role as God's lighthouse, will cast its beam along the pathway of life. Hence the reason that one of the marks of the outpouring is the great increase of souls who walk out of darkness into the marvelous light of the Kingdom of God.

Moreover, note that, in this season, God is empowering the Church to break into areas of communication which have long been monopolized by those who pride themselves as the shapers of the thinking and culture of mankind. Beyond the use of the printed pages in the form of tracts, magazines, books, and beyond leased time on radio and television, for communicating the gospel, the Church now owns and operates powerful radio stations and worldwide television networks that beam the good news of the Kingdom to every nation of the earth. In addition to this, the Church now has an ever-expanding presence on the World Wide Web in the form of websites, which use streaming audio and video to transmit worship services, crusades and conferences twenty-four hours per day. Now, one can even see and hear the gospel via cell phone. What an expansion of the coverage of the light beam from

God's lighthouse—the Church! Truly, the great commission to go into the entire world and preach the gospel is being fulfilled.

Additionally, there is a breakthrough that parallels any of the above, as far as world impact is concerned. The Church has now broken into the movie industry. Recent releases such as "One Night With The King", "The Apocalypse" and 'The Omega Code" have actually made it to the top ten list of the Box Office, within the first few weeks of their premiere. Hollywood has had to stop and take notice of the widespread public interest and appeal that these movies have generated. They are puzzled as to why storylines that are Bible-based and devoid of the proliferation of sex, violence and deceit, which is the common fare coming out of Hollywood, can make such an impact. What has also befuddled them is the low budget that the producers had at their disposal and yet were able to produce films of such high quality.

The truth is that Hollywood's movers and shakers, in dire need of positive direction, are now looking to the Church and the Bible, which they once despised. Film stars are now getting saved and are not ashamed to say so. In fact, there are those who are disposed to refuse roles in movies that espouse anti-Christ sentiments, even though the price tag may be high. I prophesy that the trend will continue until the writers and directors of Hollywood's films see the light and clean up their acts, because of difficulty to find top actors to play dirty roles. The top actors will be lining up to do movies that spread the light of the gospel of the Kingdom.

Yes, the world is being forced to stand and take notice. The Church is rapidly coming into maturity. We will let our light shine so that the world will see the good workmanship that Christ, the Master Builder, is crafting upon us. Those power brokers who occupy the citadels of power can no longer shoo us away, nor should they hope that we will slink back into our corner or sink into some dark hole, ashamed to show our face. We are like the new born baby: too large to go back up the birth canal to fit into a womb that has shrunk to a size that is too small to accommodate it. We are loosed and loving it!

The anointing fire, which has come with the out pouring, has set us aglow, as the city that sits on a hill. We cannot be hidden, even if we tried to do so ourselves. We are the veritable lighthouse of God, mandated to open the eyes of the understanding of those who have been set upon by spirits from the Kingdom of darkness. We will not put our light under a bushel any more.

Like insects drawn to a light in the window, on a dark night, the gentiles will stream into the Church. They are coming, driven by a passion to worship the True and Living God and loaded with an enthusiasm to serve. They are highly educated and they are bringing resources with them-financial, material and otherwise.

This is what the Church has been waiting on, for eons—to break into areas, which were, hitherto, deemed forbidden grounds for us. The gates to the hallowed grounds of gold and diamond mining, petroleum drilling, cruise ship operations, manufacturing and sports team ownership and/or sponsor ship, just to name a few, must open and let us in. We will shed light on doing business the Kingdom way, guided by the principles of honesty, diligence and fair play.

The intense glow that will radiate out of the Church, in this season of the outpouring, will not only cast its beam earthward. It will also send a clear signal heavenward, testifying to the fact that the bride of Christ has joined with the Spirit to say,

"Even so, come now, Lord Jesus! We are ready to be raptured into your glory. The anointing fire has smoothened out all the kinks in our armour, like a hot iron does to the wrinkles on a linen garment. We have forgiven all our abusers. We hold no grudges, prejudices or anger towards one another. We have, in all honesty, set our house in order. We are becoming the glorious Church, enveloped in a glory that is far greater in radiance and coverage than that of the former."

In response, we will hear God thunder from Heaven, with a voice that sounds like the blast of a trumpet "Come up hither! All things are ready, come to the feast. All Heaven has been waiting on your arrival." Then, in the same manner as we have been living here, enveloped in His glory, we will leave this earth, in a blaze of glory, á-la-Elijah, to meet our King and Lord, in a cloud of His glory. And all God's people say,

"HALLELUJAH! SO LET IT BE, LORD! SO LET IT BE!"

WHAT NEXT!

Obviously, Satan will not stand by idly, and allow the Church to emerge from the shadows of history to take up its God-ordained position on the centre stage of world affairs. Expect him to try his utmost to push us back; embarrass us or, at least, get us embroiled in so much in-fighting that we lose focus on what is important: the projection of a clear picture of Jesus, standing in the midst of a united Church, ablaze with his glory. He will be using a thousand and one devices, which may range from witchcraft to sickness to violence to scandals, just to name a few.

To our great advantage, though, God knows every one of Satan's plans and does have the relevant counter measure to foil it. Apostle Paul verifies this truth in 2 Corinthians 2:11, when he admonishes us not to despair in the face of impending attacks from the forces of darkness because, we are not ignorant of Satan's devices. Consequently, God is arming His Church to the teeth with every conceivable weapon of war in the Spirit. He is intent on not only having us retain what we have obtained, but also, on having us seize more territory from the Kingdom of darkness, which we will commission for His glory.

With such foreknowledge of what is to come, every one of us should strive to enter boldly through the open door, which leads to that state of being called, 'THE OUTPOURING'. There, we will live in the perpetual flow of the rivers of living water that gush from beneath the throne of God. The Spirit of God will be our life coach as we move steadily into a dimension of living called the Zoë life. Therefore, it is time for the true warriors to arise with a new sense of militancy. In this season, ONLY THE STRONG WILL SURVIVE!

THANK YOU JESUS!

Appendix

Here is a prophecy, concerning what God has decreed for the Caribbean. Yet, I feel a compulsion to deliver it to the world at large. Consequently, I have decided to append it to this book, which will become the vehicle that brings it to every continent on the globe. The world must know of this prophecy because the waves that it will generate at the point of fulfillment will wash up on the shores of even the smallest nation in the remotest part of the planet. When someone would ask, "What is the meaning of this?" the informed will reply, "A tsunami of God's glory has hit the nations of the Caribbean and the world is feeling the effects of its backwash!"

THERE IS A TSUNAMI OF GOD'S GLORY HEADING FOR THE CARIBBEAN

There is a tsunami of God's glory heading for the Caribbean. God has earmarked the nations whose shores are washed by the Caribbean Sea, as the staging area for the next major outpouring of His glory. Prophets and intercessors in this area have known it for several years and have been nurturing it in the womb of their spirits. Know, then, that the pregnancy has come to full term. The waters have bro ken. I hear the sound of huge, swift moving waves of anointing coming ever so closer to this area.

The truth is that many who have been expecting this new move are already feeling the effects of the preliminary waves. They are testifying of the rise of a greater passion for the presence of God within their inner man. They are experiencing the manifested presence of God during worship services. Prophets are becoming more accurate in the proclamation of the mind of God. Rich revelation of the word is flowing on a greater frequency. There is a greater sense of camaraderie and networking among those who have hooked up to God's prophetic frequency. Yes, the tsunami of God's glory has begun to hit the Caribbean.

When the flow becomes fully established, it will trigger a phenomenon that can only be dubbed 'Gospel Tourism'. People will come from distant shores, drawn, not by the customary pull factors - sun, sea and fun - for which this region is known, but to see how we do Church. God will use the children of former slaves and of former indentured servants to demonstrate to the children of former slave traders and colonial masters the true passion and commitment to Kingdom worship, selfless service and holy living that He desires. He no longer wants us to despise ourselves because we may be small in size and lacking in resources.

Although many of these nations of the Caribbean may not show up on maps of the world, we will certainly register as a bright spot on the spiritual radar screens of those who desire more from God. They will feel a compulsion to journey in our direction to find answers to the question—Can any good thing come out of the Caribbean? The answer will resonate across the oceans, borne on the crests of mighty waves, "Oh Yes! Come and see!"

The good news is that one does not have to be resident in the Caribbean, at present, to be at the forefront of this move of God. As long as one is of Caribbean stock, one is in line to become washed by this tsunami. Therein lies the vast potential of this move.

It has been said that there may be more Caribbean people living in foreign lands than those actually living in the Caribbean. Can you imagine the world wide Church quake that will take place? It will trigger a Jesus Revolution, when, in the USA, Japan, Australia, Canada, England, Africa, India, Europe, South America, among others, those of Caribbean stock begin to manifest the power that comes with the outpouring?

There is one caution, though. This tsunami of God's glory is not the sweep-over-all type. Rather, it may be only accessed by individuals who have taken steps to position themselves properly. It is similar in essence to what Christ had John write to the Church at Laodicea, in Revelation 3:20, TEV, "o Listen! I stand at the door and knock; if anyone hears my voice and opens the door, I will come into his house and eat with him, and he will eat with me."

The implications are serious enough for both individuals and entire ministries, not just to stop and take heed of what is happening, but also, to be responsible enough to implement radical change. Here is a short list of a few of them:

- It is my personal responsibility to prepare myself for the tsunami.
- Many ministries in the Caribbean may remain dry on the corporate level, even while individuals within, become enveloped in the tsunami.
- There may be several assemblies in the same city and even on the same street, yet, only one may flow in this new anointing, because the leader of that assembly has taken steps to open the door to the transforming power of Christ as the Revealed Word that transcends traditions and rituals.
- Positioning is everything. Where you are will determine what you receive.
- Position yourself where you ought to be and God will give you access to all the resources that you need.

In the mouths of two or more witnesses, every word is established. God has even impregnated prophets and intercessors that have little or no connection with or knowledge of the Caribbean with this same prophetic word. As recently as July 6th, 2006, God inspired Rev. Kenneth Copeland of Texas, USA, to proclaim this very word at a conference, which he was conducting. Shortly after that, God had me come into contact with two prophets from England and Wales, respectively. They both told of how God had commanded them to come to the Caribbean to observe the ever intensifying effects of the first waves of the tsunami that have already begun to hit the Church in the Caribbean and to help birth what is yet to come!

So, child of God of Caribbean stock, at home or abroad, a rise and shine. Remove the sackcloth of sorrow and the ashes of shame that came with slavery, cultural rejection and colonial domination. Put on your garments of celebration and declare God's praise in the islands and on the mainland. Whether your language is French, Spanish, Dutch, English or all the dialects in between, let your heart sing a melody of worship unto your God. He has remembered His people in the Caribbean. He has concealed us as His best kept secret, over the years. Now, He is ready to release us as polished, fiery arrows to set His Church on fire in a way that it has never experienced before.

Yours in covenant,
Apostle Vivian Duncan
Divine Destiny Worship Centre
Diego Martin
Trinidad,
West Indies

Endnotes

1 N.B. All information appearing in this segment has been sourced from issues of Charisma Magazine, produced by Strang Communications Company of Lake Mary; Florida and reproduced either through direct quotes or edited abridgements.

AUTHOR'S CONTACTS:

Apostle Emanuel Vivian Duncan

Tel: 1-868-633-3780

Email: evduncan@yahoo.com

Website: divinedestinyworshipcentre.org

www.ingramcontent.com/pod-product-compliance
Lightning Source LLC
Chambersburg PA
CBHW021442070526
44577CB00002B/252